Books should be returned on or before the
last date stamped below

- 6 AUG 2005

0 9 JUN 2012

11 JUL 2003

HEADQUARTERS

- 6 AUG 2003

0 8 JUN 2012

13 DEC 2007

- 8 FEB 2018

12 APR 2004

- 9 FEB 2008

16 NOV 2004

- 7 JUN 2008

- 4 APR 2009

29 JUL 2008

15 NOV 2008

ABERDEENSHIRE LIBRARY
AND INFORMATION SERVICE

MEL   Slaughter, Caro   RUM

Before the
knife :
memories of an
                B SLA

1468263

D0319726

Before the Knife

www.**booksattransworld**.co.uk

Also by Carolyn Slaughter

THE STORY OF THE WEASEL

COLUMBA

MAGDALENE

HEART OF THE RIVER

THE BANQUET

A PERFECT WOMAN

THE INNOCENTS

DREAMS OF THE KALAHARI

THE WIDOW

Before the Knife

MEMORIES OF AN AFRICAN CHILDHOOD

Carolyn Slaughter

Doubleday

LONDON • NEW YORK • TORONTO • SYDNEY • AUCKLAND

B SLA
1468263

TRANSWORLD PUBLISHERS
61–63 Uxbridge Road, London W5 5SA
a division of The Random House Group Ltd

RANDOM HOUSE AUSTRALIA (PTY) LTD
20 Alfred Street, Milsons Point, Sydney,
New South Wales 2061, Australia

RANDOM HOUSE NEW ZEALAND LTD
18 Poland Road, Glenfield, Auckland 10, New Zealand

RANDOM HOUSE SOUTH AFRICA (PTY) LTD
Endulini, 5a Jubilee Road, Parktown 2193, South Africa

Published 2002 by Doubleday
a division of Transworld Publishers

Copyright © Carolyn Slaughter 2002

The right of Carolyn Slaughter to be identified as the author of this work has been asserted in
accordance with sections 77 and 78 of the Copyright, Designs and Patents Act 1988.

A catalogue record for this book is available from the British Library.
ISBN 0385 603444

Lines from 'The Eye-Mote', from *Collected Poems* by Sylvia Plath, are reproduced by
permission of Faber & Faber Ltd.

All rights reserved. No part of this publication may be reproduced, stored in a retrieval system, or
transmitted in any form or by any means, electronic, mechanical, photocopying, recording or
otherwise, without the prior permission of the publishers.

Typeset in 12/17pt Granjon by Falcon Oast Graphic Art Ltd.

Printed in Great Britain by
Clays Ltd, Bungay, Suffolk

1 3 5 7 9 10 8 6 4 2

For Leita, at long last.
And for Kemp, who endured.

What I want back is what I was
Before the bed, before the knife.

SYLVIA PLATH

Acknowledgments

DURING THE LONG YEARS THAT IT'S TAKEN TO BRING THIS story to publication, many people are due my deepest gratitude. Kemp Battle, for his unfailing love and devotion, and for keeping faith at all the times that I couldn't. Leita Hamill, who read and edited every version, several times, out of friendship and without recompense, and kept right on to the end. Dan Halpern, for his kindness and contributions to the manuscript when it was first completed, and for directing me to my agent, Betsy Lerner, of the Gernert Company. She, with her glittering editorial eye, not only moulded the book into its final shape, but took it out like a lioness to the publishers. Sonny Mehta and Marty Asher of Knopf and Vintage, thank you so much for publishing this book. Marianne Velmans and Sarah Westcott, and all at Doubleday in London, your instant and affectionate response meant more to me than I can say. My children: Ally, Tom, Emily and Joe, my stepdaughter Mish, and my grandchildren, Becca, Molly and Casey, thank you for teaching me how to be a mother and grandmother. Thanks and love to other people's children who have been dear to me over the course of this writing: A. J., Doug, Fran, Frankie, Joy, Matt, Mike and Jim. Much gratitude also goes to Peggy Calvert, who became my mother the minute I arrived in America sixteen years ago. Thanks also to the many friends who have remained doggedly interested and supportive during this long incubation: Caron Avery, Anne Battle, Stephanie Beddows, Andrea Cook, Sue Cook, Logan and Ellie Fox, Kate Hughes, Liz and Sam Hynes, Shelagh Macdonald, Randi Orlando, Henry and Mary Reath, and Harriet and Geoffrey White. A particular thank you to Miriam Lowi, who, when I first told her that I was trying to write this again, said simply, just take it back to Africa, tell it how it was.

Before the Knife

Prologue

THIS IS A MEMOIR ABOUT MY CHILDHOOD IN A PARTICULAR part of Africa called the Kalahari Desert. It's about my mother and father and my two sisters and our lives in a singularly beautiful place, and it's about the childhood I happened to have found myself in, within a family that seems, at this distance, to have been as helpless about its fate as I was about my own. What happened to me affected all of us – my mother, my father, my sisters and me: we all fell apart under the horror of it, and we all tried to pretend that there was no horror. Each of us found our own way of surviving, and each of us got through alone. On the surface of it, we were what we appeared to be: an ordinary English family living in a very remote part of southern Africa during the lingering last years of British colonial rule. Our life was much like the lives of everyone else's around us and we thought and behaved as the English did at that time. No one questioned our behaviour, either in the country we had stolen from its natural owners, or in the quiet, secret rooms of our daily lives. And because everything was so orderly, there was nothing to point to and say, that was the moment it all began to decay.

All my life, I'd believed that that moment came for me when my younger sister was born because, with her birth, my shifting and tenuous connection to my mother was broken and we were never properly attached again. My older sister and I were sent off to boarding school and I had something of a breakdown, but as it turned out, those events were merely a small part of it, because the moment when everything changed only really came the night that my father first raped me. I was six years old. This rape, and the others that were to follow, obliterated in one moment both the innocence of my childhood and the fragile structure of our English family life. We all knew. I showed my mother all the proof she needed, and my older sister was right there in the room with me, in the bed across from mine. But once it had happened, we decided that it had never happened at all. In our privileged and protected world, we chose to bury it, we put it out of sight and memory, never said another word. This silence wasn't disturbed for decades, and though it was a silence that destroyed us, each in our own way, that isn't the story I want to tell.

When I lived in Africa, the great plains and deserts stretched as far as you could see, wild beasts roamed the vast savannahs, tracing and retracing their paths across ancient migration trails, moving to and from water, decay and death. On the grasslands and at the edges of the deserts, the black man lived and reigned as he had for all eternity: tilling his small fields, slaughtering his cattle and goats in times of plenty, starving or dying out when the rains didn't come, or when marauding tribes from over the hill brought his days to an end. Women pounded the maize, stirring black pots over wood fires that sent up small blue columns of smoke that vanished into the clear blue air. Sweet potatoes and fat speckled pumpkins hugged the brown earth, and under mimosa trees with spikes long as a child's finger they fed their babies and shooed chickens from underfoot, waiting for their men to come back from the bush. When the sun rose in the morning, little boys shook out their limbs and led goats out to graze, trailing sticks in the sand and wandering silently through a shorn landscape dotted with thorn bushes, interrupted only by a solitary acacia tree with branches laid flat across a sky as endless and blue as the sea.

But then one day, into this eternity we came marching. We sailed across the Atlantic, tall masts and white sails brilliant in the sunlight, and announced that we'd discovered Africa. We took a quick look around and, picking up the four corners of the sleeping continent like a picnic cloth, we shook it up, cut it into pieces and flung it back down in our own image. White faces radiant in the sun, we brought in our columns of mercenaries, our guns and whips; we spread our diseases and plagues, and toppled the landscape and the languid people who'd lived on it since time began. We stayed on for a while, sojourning in Africa the way we had in India, never really intending to stay, dreaming always of England, and those blue remembered hills. But, for all the coming and going of white feet, the snatching of lands and lakes, and all the ivory, gem, gold and trophy collecting, and the buildings of farms and cities, in the end it was always a short visit: white men coming to make a hurried living along the beautiful acres of the equator that stretch all the way up into the snow-peaked crests of mountains put down a few hundred million years ago. We took what we needed and packed up again, and in no time at all, the life of the white man, so transitory and scattered, so greedy and impatient, would be over: one by one, nation by nation, we pulled up and went back over the sea, and once we'd gone it was as if we'd never been. We left no memory of ourselves on the still air, no trace of our footsteps on the scorched plains – we were gone – no more than a handful of bleached bones on the lap of a continent that could remember man's first startled smile.

One

I WAS GOING TO SAY THAT MY FIRST MEMORY OF OUR LIFE
in Africa was at Riley's Hotel in Maun, at the top of
Botswana, on the edge of the Okavango Delta. But that isn't
so. It's just that I tend to skip over the first place we lived in,
as if I'm still trying to forget it the way I did then. That way,
for a short while, it can seem, just like the first time, somehow, not to have happened at all. Old defences rush to the
rescue so that even now, whenever I think of our life in
Africa, I go directly to the Kalahari. I blot out the years from
three to six, when my mother and I were like the first finger
and thumb of a glove that held me safely in place in the
world and gave her a measure of safety that was taken from
her just as suddenly and shockingly as it was from me.

Our life in Africa actually began in Swaziland – a tiny
African kingdom held in the fist of the Republic of South
Africa. At that time, the British government's district

commissioners oversaw the colony, and my father was sent out from England to be one of those men who strode around wearing the hard hats, khaki uniforms and knee-length socks of the Empire. We'd come out on the boat, and since I was only about three and a half at the time, I'm not sure how much I remember of that first sea voyage out. I seem to see the boat pulling out of the dock at Southampton and the paper streamers connecting, for those sad, fleeting moments, those on the boat to those on the shore. I seem to see my grandmother and my aunt far, far below, standing on the quay, stout women wearing dark clothes. My grandmother was bitter and silent when we said goodbye; she would barely kiss us and her face was stiff with anger. She'd been through all this before: my father had run off to India when he was twenty, leaving her and Ireland behind, vowing never to return to the miserable, rain-soaked poverty. Now he was at it again, taking us into another exile – this time into the dark, godforsaken hell of Africa.

My sister and I were born in India around the time of Partition and Independence, which came in 1947, and at the time of our births my grandmother had reached her determined hand across the ocean, and insisted we be baptized as Catholics. My father – deep hater of priests and the Holy Roman Church – handed us over like a lamb. Now he was trying to get away from his mother again, only this time he was escaping to Africa, and this time he wasn't going alone – he was taking my mother, my sister and me with him.

After the British had pulled up stakes from India and

headed home to England, my father hadn't been able to settle along with the rest of them. At that time, England's overseas colonies, apart from India, were held firmly under imperial domination. You had only to glance at an atlas to see how much of the world was painted red, the scarlet mark of British conquest and possession, the boot on the neck of the dispossessed. This red rash had once covered the whole of India and Pakistan, great chunks of the Near, Far and Middle East, East and Southern Africa, Australia, New Zealand and the British islands of the Caribbean, not to mention that inflamed wound on the northern tip of Ireland. And all of this vast Empire was somehow, quaintly, thought of simply as England, a frontier that stretched as far as destiny was wont to go.

India, in getting rid of the Empire, and splitting off Pakistan, had covered herself with a different kind of red. My parents, who had met and married in India, had to get out with the rest of the British and make way for in-dependence and freedom. For England and her Empire, it was the death knell, the beginning of the end, worse even than the uppitiness of the wretched Boers in South Africa who'd tried the same thing some fifty years before. In India the dream died hard. English emotions were wrung at the death of the Raj. With India gone, the Empire began to sink down into the sea. In a dozen or so years, as the red faded to pink, the imperial shade would be no more than a sign of decadence and corruption. Sharp new colours and brave flags now began to flutter over colonies where once the British had played polo and instilled a certain kind of order and gentility that was better suited to Oxfordshire or Surrey.

This giddy last fling of India under the Raj had got into my father's blood. As a young man, he'd found himself with complete dominion over more than a thousand Indians, and he'd liked it. The son of a policeman, born into poverty in Ireland in 1914, he'd found in this remote but exquisite satellite of the British Empire a place to exercise a deep need for power. It was a heady time in India, with insurrections and sectarian uprisings stirring the hot winds of independence. In Europe the war was raging, but my father was out of it. In India he'd joined the British Police, and later the Intelligence Bureau in New Delhi, where he and my mother were married and my sister and I were born. On his watch, a mighty nation was torn into two bleeding halves, and with Independence the British were thrown out, and he with them. Before you knew it, British India was no more.

When India blew up, the explosion sent the English home in ships. They left in droves – all the bureaucracy, the government officials, the businesses, hospitals and churches, the British Army and the British Police – the whole bang shoot – out. They left behind them a massive barracks of soldiers who had valiantly gone wherever they were told to serve: in the Crimea, the Americas and all the military skirmishes in Africa and Asia, as well as on the bleak battlefields of both world wars. What England expected of her officers and subjects was courage, and what she got in exchange was conquest on the cheap. What a sad business it was: left behind was a mighty structure, law and order forged out of anarchy and barbarism. Left behind them also were their lovely houses drenched in bougainvillaea and frangipani, and their cool verandaed cottages high in the hills. All the English furniture they'd carted with them over the Indian Ocean was shipped home, along with the silver, crystal and china, and the traces of Indian life, the accumulated diamonds and emeralds, the carved mahogany tables and chairs, the tiger skins, the beautiful hand-sewn clothes that we all wore. They took with them their whole way of life and they left in an orderly manner. When the flag came down for the last time, there was no lack of dignity. The British were departing, leaving behind them a job well done, a service carried out for King and Country. They left India without remorse, leaving their atrocities mingled in with the ethnic slaughters, but they knew all the same that they were being thrown out, and they couldn't quite muster up the usual resounding hoorah.

As a small girl, I remember seeing pictures of Queen Victoria's jubilees as they were celebrated in India – elephants hung with jewels, carriages carrying the Viceroy, British dignitaries and Indian maharajas and princes, tigers in cages drawn through flower-decked, cheering crowds – monarchy run amok. Now it was over and it would never be seen again, not the way it was in India, through all those long years of Victoria's reign, where her jubilees, with their glorious excess, were celebrated in Calcutta and Delhi as splendidly as they were in Westminster. The British understood pomp and ceremony – still do. Nobody does it better.

My father and mother left the opulence and beauty of India for a blitzed and shattered postwar England of rationing and meagre opportunity; they returned to the bombed cities and crippled economy of a nation still reeling from the war, shell-shocked and impoverished. It was another way of life gone to hell, and one my father couldn't take. Too depressing. What could he, in England, do with his talents for beating the natives into submission, for instilling order and respect into the barbaric hordes? He ended up in a department store in London. He stuck it out for about a year and then we were packing up again: he'd booked passage on a ship to Africa. My mother, who had been born in India and had spent her entire life there (a fact, along with many others, she didn't tell us for a long time), would have liked to stay in England, but that didn't count. My father had joined the Colonial Service; he was on the run again and we went with him, my mother, my older sister Angela and I.

The sea voyages have merged into a collective memory. The Colonial Service sent its subjects home every few years and so we sailed back and forth on majestic Union-Castle liners that bore the names of the King's houses. The elegant, blue-white ships, with crimson and black funnels, were called *Windsor*, *Dover*, or *Balmoral Castle*, and they were floating palaces, beautiful in every way. In the early days, they were part of the opening up of Africa, bringing in the mail and delivering the cargo: the cotton, the iron and steel, and the shiny new machines that were to keep the Empire running smoothly. In the holds were plants to help the emerging fruit industry in the Cape Colony, or vines to root in the fertile new land and produce brandy and wine reminiscent of Bordeaux. Ships like the ones we travelled in were part of the empire-building of a continent, bringing prospectors out to the Witwatersrand or the diamond mines of Kimberley.

The Union-Castle mail ships sailed for Africa promptly at four p.m. on Thursdays, and on their return they docked at Southampton loaded with cargo, mail and passengers just after sunrise on Fridays. So efficient was the service that people in Cape Town set their clocks by the arrival time of the mail ships. What I remember of these sea voyages is the cloudy seawater we bathed in, with soap that wouldn't lather, and scratchy white towels with a thin blue line at each end. My mother scrubbed us in a tub of salty water and poured a bucket of clear water over our heads, and then we would race down the narrow corridors in our pyjamas and back to our cabin and bed. We ate separately from the grown-ups and much earlier. We were offered hand-painted menus that announced the Children's Evening Meal. There was cereal or soup, white fish or lamb and vegetables, and always eggs to order. The main course was followed by milk pudding, jelly and cream, or ice-cream. There was always plenty of brown and white bread and butter, thinly sliced, with the crusts on. Afternoon tea was a sumptuous affair, with wafer-thin sandwiches and *petits fours* with smooth, thick white icing and a cherry or a sugared violet adorning each perfect tiny white square. Everything was served on solid silver salvers and tea was poured from pots of the same distinction.

At night the ship was lit up and the band played from the cocktail hour onwards. The grown-ups would dress up for dinner, linger over drinks served on deck and eat at tables set with delicate china, good silver and linens folded into crowns. The dining-room tables had sides that you flipped up quickly to stop the soup landing on your lap when the waves were high. A band would play and there would be dancing afterwards on a polished floor. My sister and I would sneak up and spy on the swirling couples, trying to locate our parents. My mother was the woman with the high, almost hysterical laugh. My father was the one not drinking.

During the day we raced up and down the decks, getting splinters in the soles of our feet. We would visit the engine rooms and the captain's deck, swim in the pool set like a sapphire in the dark wood deck, and play organized games the way our parents did. Everyone was kept busily engaged in ship life: there were smoking rooms, billiard and card rooms, and bars and sitting-rooms galore. Third class was a different world and one we entered surreptitiously, to slum it a bit before racing back to our posh quarters. Third class, or steerage as it was also called, was there all right, but it wasn't mentioned. Angela and I shared a cabin with two slim berths, one on top of the other. Every moment the portholes filled and emptied of blue and the water in the foldaway basin below the porthole splashed over the sides. The waves rocked us to sleep; the little cabin was a sealed world with the wind and water kept at bay. Sometimes I wondered what would happen if the hard glass of the porthole crashed and the sea came flooding in – how could we stop it? How quickly would we drown? But it would never happen: the boat was as unsinkable as our life was then. Angela slept in the top bunk and I in the one below. Sometimes her face would appear over the edge and I'd look at her upside down and laugh.

We were back in the lap of luxury. India all over again: waited on hand and foot, our every need anticipated and met. Maids, stewards and pursers replaced the ayahs, butlers and servants who'd once attended us day and night. The food was quite unlike the dreary English grub we'd left behind. The mail boats had brought with them the bounty of the southern climate, and we were eating mangoes again, and grapefruit that back then were very sour; oranges and tangerines, fat black shiny grapes, avocados and scarlet tomatoes – things unheard-of in England at the beginning of the fifties. Best of all, there were no shortages: you could eat as much meat as you liked, and meals came as frequently as they do in a sanatorium.

My mother was happy on that first voyage out. She was

the dress-up queen. I can see her long gowns hanging on the back of the cabin door on padded satin hangers. On the dressing table were her creams and cosmetics, neatly lined up, ready for war. I would test the slippery fabric of the skirt with the end of my tongue and look up at the bodice as it hung suspended, fastened by ribbons: black lace and taffeta, strapless and glamorous, tiny-waisted with full, netted underskirts that reached to the floor. Cinderella dancing shoes as transparent as glass, with small diamanté stars hanging in the icicle high heels. Mostly, when I remember her this way, I see her dancing not so much in the ship's ballroom, but on the red, polished stoep of some low-slung, ugly house in the middle of the bush, a million miles from civilization.

My mother and I began a ritual of dressing up. She loved the whole performance of getting ready to go out. She had a number of black gowns and would carefully choose which one she would wear every night. Is it too formal, she'd ask, or not formal enough? Oh, and the velvet rose is crushed and it's too late to get it ironed now. Never mind, I'll wear the satin with the low back. Be a dear and brush the black suede shoes, will you? Once she'd chosen the dress and put it on, she'd sit on a stool with the wide skirts arrayed around her, and survey her face in the mirror. Her makeup was a mask: she painted on thin, arched eyebrows, and then applied mascara from a block that she spat on and then rubbed hard with a brush. She made her mouth into an O, painted on scarlet lipstick, blotted her lips, then reapplied her smile. It would be set for the night. She would unwrap a high, flirty laugh and keep it close at hand, throwing it out when the moment seemed right. I knew this laugh didn't belong to her, and I was embarrassed that she didn't seem to know quite how or when to use it. Later on, in our house, when I heard it come flying across the room – as I walked from guest to guest offering prunes wrapped in bacon – I stiffened and winced.

But when she was adorning herself in front of the mirror she was most perfectly herself. I used to stand behind her watching her flirt with her own face. She set me little tasks like dunking the powder puff in the Helena Rubenstein box, and she let me dab silky powder on to her white shoulders. She talked fast, rattling away about the fabric of her dress and how precisely it should hang – totally absorbed in the detail of it all. She was proud of herself: my waist is still twenty-two inches small, she crooned, even after having you two. Then she glared at her teeth: they aren't as strong as they used to be, she said, you two used up all my calcium. Her voice dropped and saddened: I had beautiful teeth once, she said. Years and years later, all her teeth were capped because they'd got into such a state. The new teeth gave her a new mouth and she looked disturbingly different. Her eyes were a watery blue, her skin milky white and her cheekbones very high. Her hair was reddish blond and she wore it short, swept up on either side of her face with a curved round fringe across her forehead.

She had a copper necklace that she loved; it had oval-shaped coins linked together in an overlapping pattern. She polished the necklace with Brasso and then got Angela and me to scrub it with lemons to get rid of the Brasso smell. When she saw herself, radiant in the mirror, the copper lighting up her milky skin, she seemed to know who she was, and she was at peace. Her face, so often touched with anxiety and doubt, would become serene: beauty was her only accomplishment and she clung to it in the same desperate way that she hung on to my father's arm entering the ballroom at night. I'd watch her face, stricken for a moment in the golden light, and then the smile would come on and the strange shrill laugh would part her scarlet lips and she'd be fine, and we could both relax.

On the boat going over, I first became aware that dressing up was her game, the way Gordon's gin was her drink. I don't know who taught her to play at dressing up, but it was a game she was prepared to play with me. She was our mother now because on the boat there was no ayah to scoop us up and take us out of the room, or push us in black prams with our cotton hats pressed down hard over our ears. On the boat she was different. I remember her walking around the decks with us and sitting with us while we had our meals in the children's dining-room. She would even bathe and dress us, comb our hair, part mine on one side and sweep it up out of my face with a slide shaped like a bow. Once when I was feeling seasick, she sat with me in a deck chair in the evening air, and we watched the stars come out, wrapped up in a blanket together, safe as houses. She would read us a story at bedtime and tuck us in before she swept out, leaving the crackle and hiss of taffeta in her wake and the heady scent of Chanel No. 5. The vision in black vanished through the door and I'd press my eyes shut to keep the memory of her white shoulders and golden hair alive in my mind before, with a click of the light, she was gone and we were plunged into darkness.

We had a special bond, my mother and I; Angela belonged a bit more to my father then. There are many photos where I am close to my mother's side, her arm around me, her hand placed tenderly on my chubby arm. Angela is usually a little apart, a little stranded. I, on the other hand, am fused to her hip and she's smiling, her bobbed curls blowing in the wind. My mother had an awkward connection to Angela and it never changed. When Angela was born, it was touch-and-go for many days: after a complicated birth, Angela had emerged, bruised, weak and unable to take milk. To keep her alive, she was fed through a tube in her nose. She was perhaps too risky to love. And in time, after many disappointments, Angela began to feel the same way about our mother.

As for my father, his daughters came to him in a place where girls were deemed worse than worthless. Condolences were heaped on him the moment we entered the world, and, no doubt, had we been a darker shade, we'd have had our necks broken at birth, or our spines snapped, or been shoved in a clay pot to die. I can't imagine what my father would have done all day on the ship while my mother was planning her evenings. He didn't encourage friendships and he didn't play organized games. He was a man who felt at a loss if he couldn't be driving a car, or a plane; he had to be doing something and would often snap at us in irritation: why aren't you doing something? You'll never get anywhere if you sit around doing nothing. He learned to fly in Africa and owned a Tiger Moth, and the engines of planes and cars were of endless fascination to him all his life. Quite how he entertained himself on board is hard to imagine. Perhaps he spent hours in the engine room watching the huge machines. He liked to understand how mechanical things worked, but he wouldn't have asked questions; he'd have just figured it out, aloof and splendid in his isolation. He'd have stood and observed the black-greased sailors making the machines ignite and roar and not spoken one word. As he crossed the great ocean, and moved between one world and the next, he might have passed muster on the great machines, strutting up and down like one inspecting troops in the belly of the ship, but he'd have done this to avoid noticing that he himself was in limbo, alone on a wide, wide sea, going somewhere made not of water, but of sand.

These voyages took fourteen days, with one stop at Madeira or Las Palmas. Here we all got off the boat and were taken, jogging in rickshaws pulled by small, wiry men, to see the sights. Everyone loaded up with embroidered linens, straw baskets and huge porcelain-faced dolls with eyes that opened and shut. Back on the boat, there was a sense of expectancy, of being nearly there. We watched the moon make its daily changes. There were no birds and there was nothing in the sky as we slowly approached the southern hemisphere and left the clouds behind. We turned our faces to Africa; we could barely wait. On and on we sailed, and as the days passed, the climate and the light changed. It got hot and the air became clear as gin; shadows grew starker and the swell of the sea wilder, the colour more aqua than blue. The lovely lines of the ships, the majestic white of the hull, parted the high waves as, drawn south by some magnet, we were pulled inexorably towards Africa. We were drawing closer to the Cape, the turning point for the East and the old spice routes, the crossroads between the old world and the new.

One day, dramatically, just when we reached the equator, the entire crew down to the last man appeared in the morning light arrayed in pure white. Gone were the dark, heavy uniforms, the black polished shoes and charcoal suits and waistcoats. In their place – whiteness from top to toe – sparkling, starched uniforms with a touch of gold braid, shoes and gloves spanking white. It seemed that the higher the sun rose in the sky, and the closer we came to Africa, the whiter those white men became.

In the fifties, sailing from England to Africa on those great old liners, there was a ceremony called Crossing the Line. A King Neptune, done up in robes and beard, with trident and mitre, presided over the ceremony, which took place when the ship crossed the equator. I'm not quite sure what we as children actually did, but if you'd not crossed the equator before, you were covered in a mixture of flour and water paste and had eggs broken over your head. But one year, when I wasn't so little, something else happened. I was wearing one of those bathing suits of the time – cotton bunched up with elastic stitching into small squares – the effect like bubble-pack, only softer. Neptune was sitting on the throne, with a pleasant expression behind a ratty old beard that covered all of his face bar his eyes and mouth. We kids lined up to pass him, and we certainly got close enough for me to recognize Neptune as my father. I looked at him, and he looked at me. He was checking to see if I recognized him. I gave no clue. He gave no sign that he recognized me either. We merely exchanged glances and then we both looked quickly away. The fact that he was both Neptune and my father disturbed me. He'd become someone else, but he was still my father. Later on, as he was dressed in his normal clothes again, behaving the way he normally did, reading a paper, I didn't say that I'd known it was he. To do so would have broken a code, and I'd learned, like the rest of my family, never to break the code.

Two

AFRICA WAS SMALL POTATOES AFTER INDIA. ONCE A destination for second sons, hopeless cases and decadents, now it was merely a watering hole for colonials needing somewhere to go. Swaziland, where we went first, comes back as a lush, gardened place. The British had created Surrey there and the houses were cool and comfortable, with flower prints on the walls, good china and linens on the shelves, and silver pots for tea. There were servants in plenty to keep things functioning smoothly. The gardens had beds of roses and hollyhocks, delphiniums, lupins and sweet peas. And if there was nothing very African about the British quarters there, there was also nothing very war-like about the Swazi king. He and the British officials worked out things in an amicable manner. Hlatikulu, where we lived, and Mbabane, the capital, were both well supplied with markets, a butcher, a few shops and even a hospital and convent. We had a house there, but I can tell you nothing about it except that it had a cupboard in which one day I was horrified to come across a pram – one of those black, sailing-boat varieties. I took Angela to see it. We were puzzled. No one had mentioned anything about a baby. Soon afterwards, a friend of Angela's told us that my mother was pregnant. She must have been noticeably so, but neither of us remember that. I was six then and Angela eight.

It was in Swaziland – for reasons now abundantly clear – that my mother entered a depression from which she never got free. All my life I'd believed that her unhappiness was connected to my sister's birth: a postpartum depression. My sister's birth began, so I thought for many, many years, the emotional derailment of my life, and of my mother's: neither of us seemed able to recover. Of course, had it simply been a postpartum depression, she would have recovered from it, but she never did, and nor was she able to properly care for me again.

Up to this time, my mother had been doing just fine in Swaziland. It wasn't too different from what she'd been used to in India. The garden and cocktail parties continued, nice frocks could be worn, people were congenial and social, and Swaziland itself was close to a part of Africa that was civilized. She could go to Jo'burg, where there were shops to buy clothes and makeup, and we took trips along the coast and saw another part of Africa, and stayed in good hotels and swam in the sea.

All of Africa around us then was held tightly in white hands, so much so that, unless you were looking closely, you could pretend that the country had lost its natural and unruly strangeness, its sudden and inexplicable violence. The British weren't going to put up with any of that nonsense, and with their bureaucracies and administrations they felt sure they could make it go away. Trouble was, the violence and strangeness kept popping up, reminding us that Africa couldn't be tamed, and that the land itself, so deeply ingrained in the soul of its people, simply could not be conquered or possessed. You felt this, the hopelessness of the British endeavour, in the indifference of the landscape and in the disdainful sidelong glance in a brown eye as the owner of it stooped to pick up your dropped shoe.

In Swaziland my mother laid out her vegetable garden, worked by genial prisoners from the local jail. She got the gardeners to rake out the rocks and fold in the manure and put up neat white fences. She and I planted carrots, peas and radishes, and though we tossed them in any old way, they always came up in neat lines. Things grew in Swaziland as they were not to grow for her again. The seeds came up, lettuce plants spread their delicate leaves and formed strong hearts, the tomatoes plumped on the vine and turned scarlet, the beans flowered and sprouted, potatoes and onions became sturdy and no insects got to them before we could. She tried strawberries and we ate them; she experimented with herbs and they made it to the table.

We ate food in Swaziland of a kind and quality that would not come our way again for a very long time. There was no scurvy here and our legs didn't sprout boils that had to be dressed with scalding poultices and then lanced. There was health and plenty in Swaziland and there was no savagery in the environment: at night we could sleep without lions and hyenas creeping up to the fence. There were no scorpions in teacups or crocodiles cruising in the river at the bottom of the garden. One did not open the wardrobe and find a black mamba draped around a coat hanger. In Swaziland there were animal skins on the floor and the occasional trophy on the wall, but there was no rack of guns: the massive elephant gun, the crocodile gun, the two-bore shotgun used for game, the .375 Magnum Express, and the little house gun kept beside the bed, ready and loaded, just in case. All this was coming up soon, when we reached the Kalahari.

In Swaziland, our mother handed us back to nannies with relief and planned her evening entertainment. She could spend her days complaining about the Servant Problem, and intimidated the young women who polished her furniture and floors and washed and ironed her clothes, returning them spotless at the end of each day. They tended not to look at her as she complained about an untidy crease or a loose button; they lowered their eyes in a shy and secretive manner that she thought downright surly. One of these young women was in charge of our laundry and her duties were exacting. She had to ensure that no piece of our linen – no tablecloth, hankie, napkin or white shirt – came before my mother's eye unless it was scrupulously white. If not, it would be returned to the laundry basket, and from there proceed to the sink to be washed by hand, scrubbed against a board, boiled in a vat on the kitchen stove, rinsed in water that contained a tiny blue block wrapped in muslin, and then dunked in a starch solution before it was hung out in the sun to dry. And while all this was going on in the laundry room, our cook – a man carrying the genes of the bloodiest tribe of Africa – was so scared of my mother that he sobbed in the sink each time she flung back a flopped soufflé, or a chicken that wasn't perfectly moist and tender. How many times does one have to tell them, she'd moan, not to open the oven door to see if the soufflé is rising? Why won't they ever learn? We didn't have this kind of problem in India, certainly not. Indians are intelligent people, on the whole, or at least they understand the culinary arts.

This happy state of affairs was not to last. Soon my mother would have no energy to boss the servants and no inclination to go out to tea or dress up for a garden party, because, for all its gentility, something had happened in Swaziland that no amount of washing could whiten. For another, we were about to leave Swaziland's green hills and be transferred to the desert protectorate of Bechuanaland. I don't know how soon my mother became aware of this move, but it was another factor in her decline. As it was, since she was clearly unable to cope, Angela and I were sent off to a boarding school many miles away. This school was called Goedgegun, an Afrikaans word meaning something like good-going. The move to the boarding school presented Angela and me with a bewildering first separation from our parents and an early indoctrination into the barbarities of school life.

At Goedgegun we were weekly boarders, worse than being regular boarders, because this way we were saved on Fridays only to be dispatched back to hell on Sundays to endure the week again. We couldn't speak a word of Afrikaans and we were hungry all the time. Angela learned how to crack chicken bones to suck out the marrow, something she still does. We had one portion of sugar a day, which could be taken on the disgusting lumpy mealie-meal, or brown, grainy Matebele porridge, or on the daily slice of bread. We always had it on the bread: no contest – it was pure pleasure, that single slice of sugared bread. Eating it, very slowly, redeemed the morning and let us forget for a moment what was to follow.

I'd been clean as a whistle when I arrived, but on the very first night at the school I lost control of my bladder. Every night I would sleep in the warm, loving stink of my own urine, and in the morning I'd wake to the horror and humiliation of my disgrace. Matron would be there with a string of expletives and she'd drag me off to the bathroom. She threw my sheets in the bath and made me wash them; this was hard because I could barely reach my arms to the bottom of the tub. But for all her efforts, there was nothing

I could do to stop, and I was as appalled as she was by the constancy of my habits. Stronger measures were needed: Matron took me back to the bathroom and made signs that I should pee in a basin that she'd placed on the floor. For some reason, I was now unable to produce a drop. When, finally, I did it, she poured the urine carefully into a glass and handed it to me. I thought she must be crazy, stared at her and handed it right back. She told me to drink it. Everyone knew. In the school's hierarchy of public humiliation, I joined the boy who walked the halls with a placard on his back announcing: I am a thief. I couldn't look at him: I was so terrified of his shaming and my own nearness to his condition. I could barely survive the five days of boarding before there was the short reprieve of home. Angela couldn't save me, and in despair, she took a position she was to maintain in the years to come: she looked the other way. I remember crying all the time, quietly in my bed, or openly, if I thought it would help.

When I got home, I'd be happy for the first day, and then when I'd realize I was going to be sent back to school, my sobbing started up all over again. My mother couldn't help me; she had her hands full. She would just say, you have to go, that's all there is to it. And she'd turn her back and walk away so she didn't have to look when my father grabbed me and stuck me in the back of the car. In the back seat, Angela was sitting silently, with her head down, trying to be good. She would scowl at me and hiss: Just stop screaming like that. Stop it now.

My father would sing on the way. I remember him singing 'Danny Boy' and an old Catholic tune called 'The Bells of St Mary's'. He was happy in Swaziland, he'd got his world under control again and now, with us out of the house, he thought my mother might settle down and stop feeling sorry for herself. He was back in the game – the old British game of instilling order and obedience, and of making the blacks get off their idle backsides and work. He was a man who liked a uniform; he must have missed his Indian Police getup: the jodhpurs and high boots, the jacket with flat pockets and epaulettes, the ceremonial sword for high days and holidays, and the gun in the holster at all times. He couldn't have walked around like that in the bush, of course, but he wore crisp, starched khakis and a helmet, and there were always the sharp whites for special occasions. He was in his element. The fact that England was fast losing her grip on Africa, so much so that her presence would be wiped off the map in a decade or so, hadn't settled in yet. White supremacy was here to stay.

The fact that my mother was losing her grip probably escaped his notice too. She got us out of the house and he drove us to boarding school on Sunday nights, singing. All was well. His relief in being out of that store job on Oxford Street must have been overwhelming. England had been such an unpleasant shock. It was gutted, as the Indian Empire had been gutted. He'd got out just in time. Now, in the green and pleasant enclave of Swaziland, my father and his kind could keep the drums rolling a little longer, hold the darkness at bay, and bring the benefits of civilization to those in need of a stiff rod.

While my father was setting the stage for an impressive colonial career, my mother was as miserable as sin, and I was contributing to her unhappiness. My rage about being thrown out of home was upsetting everyone but my father, who kept up at all times a formidable indifference to all of us. My mother made it clear to me that my screaming and carrying-on had to stop. But I couldn't stop. I was devastated by my mother's abandonment. The new baby with her curly golden hair and blue eyes had so little to offer in comparison to the devotion I felt for my mother. I trailed after her as she carried Susan in her arms; I offered to do things for her, and she swatted me impatiently aside. Newborn babies were considered too delicate to be handled by a black nanny, who could never be quite clean enough, and so my mother was obliged to take care of Susan all by herself. The task exhausted her. I exhausted her; my screaming when I was sent off to school was more than she could take. Just before Susan was born, she'd impressed on me that she wanted me to grow up so that I could be of help to her, so I'd moved myself right along: I'd learned how to tie my shoes and to wash and take care of myself. I couldn't have done more to grow up, but then, after the new baby's arrival – or so it seemed to me – it had all gone horribly wrong. My mother suddenly couldn't stand the sight of me, and the more I wailed and sobbed, the more she turned away from me.

I got obsessed with the notion that the intruder was the problem; it wasn't my fault that everything had gone wrong, it was Susan's. I dreamed of shoving her down the lavatory and pulling the chain. I thought of losing her in the bush or sending her out in a basket on the river, never to return. The fact that I was fond of her and wanted to pick her up and carry her around bewildered me. I was trying my best to hate her, to make her the reason for my fall from grace, but I also half knew that she wasn't. And because I was at such a loss to understand why things had changed so dramatically between my mother and me, I slowly came to the conclusion that it must be my fault.

I was flooding the sheets and mattress every weekend. I tried to hide the sheets, or make my bed so no one would see, but I was always caught. I started to suck my thumb again until it turned into a shrunken yellow worm. I had nightmares and woke everyone with my shrieking in the night. I'd beg my mother not to leave me when I went to bed. I used to clutch at her and babble that I couldn't breathe. In exasperation, she stopped coming to me when I had nightmares and left me there in the dark. I sometimes felt that I was dying. I often thought that there was a ghost in my room, someone walking across to my bed and reaching for my pillow. When morning came, I was startled that I hadn't disappeared into the darkness.

We lived in Swaziland for a long time, at least by our standards. We left when I was six so we'd been there for almost three years. I have clearer memories of school than of home life. I remember the dormitory I slept in, with the small iron beds and the scratchy grey army blankets. We made our beds with hospital corners; if you didn't get it right, you'd have to strip the bed and do the whole thing again. My hands seemed to go useless and wiggly when I tried to tuck in the sheets, whether from fear or plain simple smallness, I don't know. There was bed inspection and shoe inspection and all of it was regimentally maintained. If I sat on the bed, my feet didn't touch the ground and I remember skidding on the red polished floor and cutting my head open, which earned me some attention from Angela, but no other dispensations. This may have been the first of the accidents that just kept on coming throughout my childhood.

I have a sense that just when Angela and I were getting a little used to the horrors of Goedgegun, we were taken out of it. One weekend we got home to find that though my mother hadn't recovered, we were coming home. My mother was still listless and unhappy; our absence from the house hadn't done the trick and in a strange, subterranean way, I felt guilty about that too. There are two snapshots of this time, taken with a Brownie camera, and in both my mother's head is hanging down and her body is slumped sideways. She doesn't have the energy to lift her head and there's a deep sense of sadness about her. In one of the photographs Susan is holding a teddy bear, but by the second shot the teddy bear is in my possession. The other thing I notice is that my head is down too, and my expression matches my mother's, as if, in order to remain connected to her at all, I had to absorb her mood and make it my own.

We'd been brought home for a different reason. We were to leave Swaziland, and soon the activity of departure roused my mother from her reverie. This was a performance that happened with great regularity throughout our childhood: we'd pack up and move on. All the crates and tea chests came out; the china and glass came off the shelves to be wrapped in newspaper, the furniture would be loaded up, the curtains came down and the animal skins were rolled up and tied with string. My mother would whirl through our clothing and see which of Angela's clothes could be turned into hand-me-downs for me; my clothes were given to the black kids, and Susan would get new ones. Then our mother made an inventory of our toys and chucked out as much as she could and, once she'd made up her mind, she wouldn't relent. Sometimes packing up and moving on energized my mother; she felt she was being given another chance to start over, to be happier and more at home. She didn't feel this way about leaving Swaziland, and perhaps that was because people had told her where she was going to, and what she was getting into.

Three

WE WERE GOING TO THE KALAHARI DESERT. IT'S A LONG way from Swaziland. We had to drive across the Republic of South Africa and way up to the northern part of what was then Bechuanaland Protectorate – we called it the B.P. – it's Botswana now. Above the B.P. is Rhodesia, now Zimbabwe, and the ruins of what was once Northern Rhodesia, now Zambia. To the west is Namibia and below is the Republic of South Africa, the narrow part of the pear shape that is Africa. We headed first for the capital of Botswana, Gaberones, and then drove up the rutted and corrugated main road through places with singsong names: Mahalapye, Palapye and Serowe. When we reached the east, and Francistown, we turned off the road and drove straight into the heart of the desert, moving up towards the northern end of the Kalahari to our destination, a town called Maun. Maun is pronounced like brown, although the locals say it more like Ma-ooon.

We were taking the old route up to Maun and the delta. It's a route as ancient and formidable as the vast, empty salt pans that the road skirts, and it meanders and goes into hiding much as the river does. On and on it wearily goes, blurring the distance, lonely as the emptiness up ahead. Prehistoric creatures opened up the first paths, making their way to water along migration trails older than history. Elephant, wildebeest, buffalo and impala herds gave it its first imprint, their spoor leaving a trace that the sand blew over, but couldn't quite eradicate. The first human footprints were the Bushmen's, who followed these instinctive lines leading to water and to game; and this half-forgotten, half-remembered track led the first white men to the same promised oasis at the end of the road. Slowly a highway emerged from the loose, shifting track as wagons, driven by white hunters and Indian traders, smoothed over the grasses in their path. And then the domesticated animals followed, the cattle that managed to thrive on the desert grasses that grew in abundance then. We were driving on a path trodden and worn and journeyed since prehistoric days, but a great deal of the time you'd be hard pressed to see it at all.

My father managed to locate himself and stay on this elusive roadway; I presume some kind of map led us across the unsignposted sand to our destination. Occasionally there might be traces of low scrubland, or a slight rise or fall in the plain. I think we drove in a Land Rover, though nowadays they're all Land Cruisers and 4x4s. Looking back on it, it's hard to imagine anywhere that my mother was less suited to. The road disappeared into rolling banks; the sand tyres moved listlessly through thick swathes of sand, sometimes wallowing and frequently getting stuck. Though there was no more than a track, to move off it – diverted by a mantle of sand that looked less deep and dense – was fatal. The track had always been there, it contained the memory of water; if we left it, we'd have been lost in no time and dead in days.

When you drive through the Kalahari, there's barely a tree or a rise; there's nothing but a bleached-out view up ahead of you and a stunning silence. The air is so clear that objects miles away seem close and sound travels in a peculiar way, feeling close to you too. The sunburned plains shimmer beneath the blue African sky and you feel that you'll never reach the horizon. Occasionally you come across the rivelled carcass of a buck or the ghost of an elephant. As you sit there at the wheel, you become part of an infinite world, a dream world so beguiling that you're tempted to fall asleep and never wake up.

We drove on into the centre, skirting the edges of the Makgadikgadi Pans: glittering, ancient salt pans haunted by the memory of what was once a vast lake watered by the great Zambezi River. Now it's empty and silent as the mirages making waves across shores once lapped by blue water. The lake has forgotten what the land remembers, but each time the rains come, the pans go back to what they once were; they become blue overnight and the flamingos return, turning the blue to pink and bringing the enigmatic lake beds back to life. Then, in a matter of weeks, the flamingos are gone – their breathless beauty vanishes, as if, like all nomads, they know precisely when to leave.

We'd come to a place inhabited by nomads since the beginning of time. Behind us shimmered the memory of India, lost for ever, and England, a place cold and un-welcoming to my father, an Irishman, and merely a fantasy to my Indian-born mother. Behind us, too, was the little England of Swaziland, and what had happened there. So there we were, with no home to call our own, and nowhere to return to, in the middle of the bush, our fate entirely in the hands of a man who'd hooked his domestic imperialism on to an empire founded on robbery and war, at a time when the natives were beginning to get restless. We took on our own nomadic life, moving through the Kalahari Desert from one dusty British outpost to the next, sometimes stay-ing no longer than six months in any one place, always moving on; always leaving something behind us, and if we turned our heads to look back, like a mirage, suddenly it had vanished.

When my father drove us to the Kalahari, he was taking us farther into the interior and, as far as my mother was concerned, even farther from civilization and hope. We were on our way to our first posting, at the most remote part of the desert, heading for Maun. My father would have quite liked making the trip; the disappearing, almost invisible road would have been a challenge, something he could get the better of. He called our attention to the giraffes gliding with their heads in the clouds, or, when he became excited by a herd of springbok cantering off into the distance, he'd turn and yell in exasperation: Why don't you bloody well look at anything? We two, Ange and I, lay drooping in the back, stuck to the seat, exhausted by glare and heat, barely able to lift our heads.

In the front seat, my mother was having a nightmare. Around her she saw nothing but sand, heat and glare, nothing to shield her, nothing to entertain her, nothing to help her forget where she was headed. As my father kept pointing out the wild game, my mother sank lower into her seat. She didn't give a damn about the zebras stepping delicately across the mirage up ahead; even a solitary lion disgusted her, and orders about what she should be looking at out of the window were making her furious. She wouldn't speak. She wouldn't look. I can see her now because I knew her so well. I'd begun to study her every gesture and movement as if my life depended on it. I could anticipate her mood, I knew what she was thinking, and I knew what she was feeling. She was crying and thinking that none of us knew that. She stared out of the window, seeing nothing, not even the bones and relics of earlier travellers, not even the ghost of a shoreline left on the sand.

Driving through the desert a numbing inertia creeps over the body and the need to sleep becomes overpowering.

The head wilts and the eyes close, but my father stayed alert at all times. I can't imagine him taking a driver, as a more normal person would have done. He would do it his way and his way was the right way. He kept driving until the destination was reached; he was at the wheel and we as passengers were simply cargo. My father's impatience and determination collided with my mother's mounting and silent despair, making the thick air static and volatile. The strain of it was unbearable. We children endured both with utmost misery, trapped in the Land Rover, waiting it out, knowing that our father would stop when he got there and not before.

When you've been out in the middle of the desert for an hour or so, your skin and hair turn stiff with dust; your mouth and lips parch and crack. The glare and the hot air blowing through the windows leave a film over everything; insects come from nowhere and settle in your eyes or splatter on the windscreen. A mass migration of butterflies can swirl around you for hours, blocking out the light, and the animals at noon go very still so it's as if life is suspended in a liquid gel. It's hard to breathe and impossible to think. The mind wanders; it starts to loop back on itself, arranging and rearranging its images, making no sense, finding no order. My mother sat as if sleeping, her head slumped over Susan's head, rallying herself to stick a bottle in Susan's mouth from time to time. She opened a small flat blue tin of Nivea Cream and dabbed it on her lips, again and again, feeling it melt and join with the sweat above her top lip. She said not a word. Soon my father's strange joviality dried up and his hands gripped the wheel as if to choke it.

This went on for days. At night, we couldn't get out and make camp or we'd have been eaten by daybreak. In the morning, my mother got out of the Land Rover and cleaned her teeth from a tumbler of water; we looked at the precious water draining into the sand and stood back as my father exploded. My mother ignored him, turning her back, spitting. I looked at her; at a hundred and five degrees she'd turned to ice. We ate some dry rations and on we went. The day stretched endlessly before us, the heat built up and the dust blew in the windows, and pretty soon I was vomiting out of the window again. This habit of mine drove my parents crazy, angering my father particularly because he disliked anything hitting the side of the car, or making a mess inside it. I used to look back and watch the vomit blowing away in the wind. When my head was back in, Angela would dig her elbow hard in my ribs and hiss, stop it, as if I could.

At the end of this journey, we reached the world's largest and most spectacular oasis. Maun lies at the tip of the Okavango Delta, where the Kalahari sand meets a trail of sweet water that's come on a miraculous journey from the mountains of Angola. The floods begin in spring and travel down through swamps and waterways to end up quietly on the shores of this little town. I remember Maun for the beauty and tranquillity of its landscape, but it was a different matter for my mother. As she saw it, my father had dragged her half across the world and through a hellish desert only to land her in a god-awful place that didn't even have a town. It had a name for a town, but no town, it had no shops – no grocery store, no chemist, no butcher, no baker, no hospital, no doctor, no dentist, no garage, no library, no post office, no bank, no petrol station – nothing, miles and miles of nothing. What it did have was plenty of disease: malaria, typhus, pneumonia, dysentery, sleeping sickness, tuberculosis, diphtheria, smallpox and polio. And every conceivable wild animal, serpent and creepy insect imaginable.

Of course it had a hotel. All the little settlements, some of them having no more than ten European houses, had a hotel. Hotels in remote protectorates were peculiar to themselves. They were there to accommodate visiting civil servants coming for a spell: a vet to study the tsetse fly or cattle, or a dentist or doctor who would fly in to do the six-month checkups made available to Her Majesty's servants out in the bush. We stayed at Riley's Hotel in Maun, which lies close to the Thamalakane River, because there was nowhere else for us to live when we first got there. It was a flat, long building with beautiful gardens watered by the river; tall frangipani trees dropped creamy flowers that had the scent of honeysuckle, only sweeter and more cloying. Scarlet bougainvillaea cluttered the walls; passionflowers and their purple, wrinkly-skinned fruit – what we called granadillas – tumbled together with roses and iris and lotus flowers. It was under these trees that Angela and I played, making our houses in the shade, drunk on the fragrance of the frangipanis. There were pawpaw and banana trees off to the side and a swing behind the hotel. Here we would play ghosts – Angela and me. We would run into the wet linen hanging on the clothes lines and see our gummed shapes appear, and our mouths and eyes disappear, becoming white hollows. The African women would run out across the scuffed earth and shake their arms at us, shooing us away like chickens. Sometimes they'd give up and yank the sheets off the line, dropping them into baskets to take them into the hot kitchens. We would trail after them, watching them spit on the black irons before thumping them down on the linen sheets as they turned them into immaculate white squares.

Angela found a friend immediately in Barbara Riley, who was the daughter of the hotel owner. Barbara showed us around and told us stories of the legendary Bobby Wilmott, who shot crocodiles in a manner surpassed by no other, but who in the end died not in the jaws of a croc, but by the bite of a black mamba. She took us to the little room where we would go to school with the rest of the white kids. Here we were all shuffled together to pick up what we could of the rudiments of reading, writing and arithmetic. This was the beginning of an education coming out of bush schools; our lessons would be conducted either in a room in someone's house, or in a small building used as a schoolroom. There weren't many of us kids, and it didn't matter much if we were different ages; we learned what was being taught that day and did the best we could, as did the teacher, Mrs Kotse. I seem to hear rather than see the schoolroom; it comes back with singing spilling out of an open door, children's voices singing 'Jan Pierewit' and 'Sarie Marais'. Mrs Kotse, a blond, striking Afrikaans woman, taught us songs that I remember to this day. I also remember her mouth: she had a tiny pearl of spit that never left her lips; it moved, as she spoke, from top to bottom lip, and when she sang it moved all the quicker, but since it never seemed to go, it was fascinating to watch it move.

I was taught to read mainly by my mother, who had Peter and Jane reading manuals from England. We'd sit on the red-tiled stoep in the afternoons, and I'd struggle with: See Rover run. See Jane run. See Peter run. Peter tended to have a more active and interesting life than Jane, who was kept pretty much in the kitchen with her mother. My mother tried to be diligent with these lessons, but she was restless and impatient, eager to get rid of me, but since reading gave me a little time alone with her, I strung it out, and that made her more impatient. Years later, in England, as a mother myself, I taught my children to read from these same reading books, which hadn't changed an iota in the interim.

Angela and Barbara Riley inhabited a glamorous world of make-believe that I was too young to understand. They took great pride in their lovely dark hair and called themselves the brunettes; they whispered together under the trees and went on assignations. I was somewhat stranded, but then I discovered what I came to need and depend on far more than friendship, or love, or family. I found the river and fell headlong into its deep mysteries. The Okavango River, of which the Thamalakane at Maun is a part, threads its way slowly and mysteriously through the desert of northwest Botswana, slowly building up flood-water. As it wends its way down, it transforms everything in its path. The desert turns green, the grasses and veld flowers make a flashy appearance, ducks, geese and partridges fill the air, the doves coo in the treetops. Villagers wait anxiously for news of its progress, listening for the drums as the floodwater slowly builds and journeys south, starting at Shakawe and moving down a string of towns. They become exuberant and noisy when it's on the way; they oil their bodies and bring out the cooking pots. The river is coming back. Life has returned. No drought this year.

It's a strangely unnatural river. The floodwater stays afloat on the sand, not seeping through, as it ought to. This is because it has a secret, unseen inner world: an underground sea of fossil water that lies deep beneath the Okavango River. The floodwater is in fact riding on top of this ancient river, enabling the new river to stay intact rather than scattering and spilling into the sand. The Okavango is peculiar, too, in that it roars down in the dry, rainless season, and it flows in channels that should widen, but instead get narrower, or clog up with sand, high reeds or dense papyrus, causing the river to disappear and re-appear entirely at its own whim. Hippo grass and pink and blue water lilies smother the waterways, choking off the water for a while. And then the river returns – a sinuous trickle of water leading into a stream, a winding labyrinth, an island, a lagoon, or a vast swamp – the hidden water bursts out of the sand and there's a river once more.

Riley's Hotel was a safer and lovelier place than home and it left me with an indelible love of hotels. My sense is that I was able to sleep in a hotel room unmolested. Angela and I had our own room, with white bedspreads and a window overlooking the back garden where the washing billowed in the wind. We had our meals early in the dining-room, and were waited on by elegant, fezzed waiters, who stood against the walls and then miraculously appeared at our elbows when their services were needed. They were kind to us, giving us extra helpings, endlessly picking our starched napkins off the floor, frowning when our manners deteriorated. They called us missy, or little missy, and occasionally even provided some gentle paternal discipline: Missy, this is not what a young girl does with her food, or, more ominously, God is not happy with the child who wastes food. The thick, creamy white china with its thin, pale green rim came to us laden with heavy, and very English, food: roast beef, roast potatoes, Yorkshire pudding and overcooked vegetables, and delicious sponge puddings covered in Lyle's Golden Syrup and served with a slick of

Bird's Custard. These stodgy desserts were identical to those served in English boarding schools. They were the shape and size of a Swiss roll, long and rounded – and if they had currants in them they were called Spotted Dick, and if chocolate, Elephant's Tool.

The only place that rivalled the river in Maun was our tree house. When we left Riley's and moved into our own house, we found – down the slope that led from our house to the river, and not far from the water's edge – a remarkable tree house. It was a huge old tree, into the arms of which a strangler fig had grown, whipping its tendrils up and over the trunk and into the limbs, slowly and quietly strangling it to death. We called the tendrils monkey ropes, and used them to get in and out of the tree, and to climb on to a flat platform at the heart of the tree that served as a room with leafy walls. The platform was the top of a vast termite mound made of ant spit and shit that had been slowly and meticulously created by these industrious ants. The wraparound termite spire was protecting the trunk of the tree from the invasive fig. If you dug into the surface, or kicked free an inner view, you could see the intricate domes, passageways and arches. As soon as a wall was damaged, the repair team moved in to patch and build again, which made the structure even stronger. We would sit up in the tree, Angela and I, happy as could be, as the African women came gliding along with jugs on their heads and babies on their backs; they would stop and smile, adjust the sleeping baby and give us a handful of guavas.

Every morning we ran down to the tree house, but we never set foot in the river because of the crocodiles cruising up and down, disguising themselves as drifting logs. Sometimes a log would slide up on to the bank and wait motionless on the warm sand. The flat, brown water was dappled with pink and white water lilies resting on green saucers. Our boat rocked among the reeds and wild duck flew, just one or two, caught up in the hot air that made everything so still, green-blue and everlasting. The water stirred, barely, the egrets stood, and a lone African child scooped mud into the pink of her hand to flatten it into a cake. Another child lunged into our kitchen, hitting her head against my nanny's belly, and ran to where the cook was kneading the bread. She pulled at his apron and gestured wildly, babbling in terror. He turned to the child who was wailing, Ai, ai, ai. My sister she is gone in the river. The word, gone, dragged her little sister down to the deeps of the riverbed. The other sister snatched at her hair, hauled at the cook's arm and pleaded, call the morena, tell him to come now-now. And the cook, his hands back in the dough, sighed and said, go home, go home, it is too late.

Every day we were told to stay out of the water: if it wasn't the crocs, it was bilharzia. Stay out of the river or be dead. I did stay out of the river, but it didn't mean you couldn't look. I would squat at the edge of the brown sullen water – it was dark, sluggish, laden with the debris of life.

You could sit in the boat and reach out to a lily pad and pull it out by the root. The green cord turned brown and then white and a smell came off it of mud and darkness, and the slow rocking of the sleepy current spoke dreamily of death. When Ange was off with Barbara Riley, I'd climb the tree and sit with my knees up, watching the river become a mirror in the still heat. I'd stare at the river's broad face, and slowly I would seem to disappear into its heavy waters. My body would vanish and I could enter the dark water, becoming one with it. I'd be carried like a child asleep on a brown bosom as on and on we'd go, deeper and deeper into the serpentine twists of the narrow channels leading into the swamps. Here, among little islands and shallow lagoons ringed by lotus leaves and wild gardenia, here, the river and I would slow and swirl and gently come to rest locked in each other's arms.

In my lost and dissolved state, I'd be startled to hear Violet's voice calling up at me, the hand-shaped leaves making shadows on her face. In her blue uniform, with starched white apron and a neatly folded doek on her head, she'd be standing looking up at me, hands on hips, her face full of annoyance. What you doing there? Up the tree like a bab-ooon? Nobody can find you. Always gone, always dreaming sitting up. Get down from this tree and come now-now. The madam is angry and you get me in bad trouble for losing you. She'd yank at my foot, or slap at my leg to get me moving. I'd come back down to earth and trail after her up the scuffed path to our house set back among mopane and acacia trees, with its green corrugated roof and flat white walls trailing scarlet bougainvillaea and creeper. As I got closer to home, my heart became twig-like and stiff. The minute I was inside, I was shut down, all my senses closed off and silenced. I moved through my outside life from a place far beyond it, barely awake, barely feeling anything at all.

The tree house and the river that lapped it had one simple lesson to teach us: learn how to survive. My mother never quite managed that. She went to the garden and tried to make vegetables grow as they'd grown in Swaziland. We were living on squash, pumpkin and sweet potatoes, but my mother wanted lettuce. She had the seeds and with the help of the gardener she planted and waited, but nothing happened: the seeds vanished, or never took root. But then she had one small but glorious success: a soft-leafed lettuce made a shoot, then a few leaves, then more, and then it became a lettuce, the real thing. My mother desperately tried to keep it alive – and lo, somehow it did survive the insects, blights and chomping creatures. She protected it with wire netting and pampered it day and night, and she would come back from the garden smiling. Angela and I didn't care about the lettuce, but it was essential that she keep smiling. When the soft green hope was full-hearted and plump, she went down to cut it, but the damn lettuce had shrivelled up overnight; it was nothing more than a green smear on the ground. She stood there and looked at it, and then walked away. We'd been intensely preoccupied with this lettuce, watching it grow, cheering it on, and when she came back from the garden with her head down, we were done for too.

Lettuce, like a great many things, could not survive in Maun. Most of our food was trucked in every few months from Rhodesia: dried goods came in bulk, and there was always quite a palaver about their arrival. When had they left Bulawayo? How far had they got? Would the sugar last, or the yeast or flour, or the little blue bags that kept the laundry perfectly white? My mother used to tear apart the packets of tea and shake out the last of the leaves so nothing was lost – something she continued to do all her life. Sugar, brown for them, white for us, came in sacks, as did salt, coffee, tea, flour, dried milk, Spam, corned beef, sardines, rice and dried beans and peas, condensed milk and Cow & Gate baby milk for Susan. Jams came in tins with the name Koo written on them, there was peanut butter, marmalade, tinned and dried fruit, sometimes little treats like jars of Marmite – all the staples, but no pasta back then and cheese a rarity. For the rest, we could manage on venison and beef, chickens, eggs, and, in Maun at least, wild duck from the river and bream and barbel, if you could put out of mind the ugliness of the fish with their hot eyes and whiskery fins, or could stomach the coarse, muddy taste of its flesh. We didn't eat the termites, but the Africans loved them – trapping them with lights as they flew out into the darkness and knocking them back like peanuts. We stared in disgust; they laughed at us and said we didn't know what we were missing.

The Afrikaner women living in Maun, a handful of that staunch and competent tribe, always had some of their stores left over when the rest of us had scoffed all ours. I'd be sent over to Mrs Kotse's for a cup of sugar or a few ounces of flour. Those Afrikaner women really knew how to cook: they made milk tarts and delicious koeksisters – a kind of plaited doughnut fried and doused with syrup; they made jam from the white part of watermelons, made our birthday cakes to any shape or design and decorated them with thick icing. They made butter and cheese and could even handle the intricacies of candle making. They hung delicious strips of venison, biltong, to dry out in the sun, made fat lengths of spicy sausages called boerewors and sent rich, tangy stews and chicken soup to anyone who was ailing or distressed.

Wherever we went in the B.P. there would be a few Afrikaners mixed in with the British – they would be part of the Public Works Department, or they were store-keepers or mechanics. They had an invaluable place in these tiny bush communities, but were treated with con-descension by the British. My mother couldn't stand them; she thought them uncouth and primitive, and in their presence she became snooty and downright rude. She'd look down at her scarlet nails, or fluff her hair – which one of them had laboriously permed, sitting on a stoep in the boiling heat – and then move off with a shrug of disdain. My mother was of the opinion that being British was enough to allow her this elevation, this and the fact that she could speak in an affected accent that she'd acquired some-where along the way. The women treated her kindly: they knew she was in trouble; in their eyes was a kind of pity that, had she been looking, she'd have been appalled to see.

Unlike us, the Afrikaners weren't putting up tents; they were there to stay. And, like their Huguenot forebears, they didn't drag France or Holland along with them when they set sail for Africa. They started over, and this allowed them to connect with the new country in a wholehearted manner that seemed seldom possible for the British. Afrikaners had no version of the British making-the-colonies-pay policy – a hit-and-run approach at best. Instead, they made Africa their home and settled it. They brought their history, their habits and their talents, but they adapted these to what was already there. They'd left Holland and France to make a new religion for themselves, and once in Africa, they allowed their language to muck in with all the other lingoes, which made for a dynamic, hybrid tongue, constantly changing. Of course, by the time we got there, the Boers had long ago beaten the British at their own game of land-snatching and were home free, beginning a new system of subjection learned first-hand from their former masters.

We kids hung around the Afrikaners' kitchens as much as possible, looking for handouts, or watching the women applying home permanents – smearing on ferocious chemicals that scalded the scalp and left hair more dead than alive. The women favoured housedresses, shapeless cotton overalls with wide sleeves and big pockets, but they made our clothes beautifully, usually in a room at the back of a prefab house set in a square of dust with skin-and-bone dogs lolling about on the back stoep. The woman who made my dresses was a middle-aged, blunt-bodied woman with curly grey hair, and her name was Mrs Brink. There were fittings in the afternoon and I remember my dresses in the same way that I remember my mother's. They had the wonderful smell of new cotton and the material was crisp and shiny. It too had come on the back of the truck. It would be thumped out, turned and rolled, and then cut with heavy scissors, the edges finished with pinking shears. The clearest memory is of standing on the kitchen table with Mrs Brink moving around me with her mouth full of pins, her head to one side. She took in a seam, adjusted the gathers, set the white collar on the neck, and went back to a whirring Singer agitated by her foot. I tried the dress on, again and again, to have the seams pulled this way and that, the bow tied at the back, the puffed sleeves pulled into alignment, the collar not quite right yet. Ag, I'll just have another try. Go into the kitchen meanwhile and get the girl to give you a cool drink.

The most beautiful of these dresses was a pale blue nylon party frock with tiny white dots all over; it had a full net petticoat underneath that was separate, and I wore it to dance around in on hot afternoons when the house was sleeping. The waist led off into tiers of stiff net, getting more voluptuously full, till by the last layer, you couldn't see your legs at all. It was a dress that took all the misery away, but some days the dress didn't work, and I'd feel filthy as a roach. In a rage, I'd attack my doll's cloth face, unpicking her scarlet mouth, pulling off her blue glass eyes and tying her long legs into a knot. Then I'd run off into the bush to huddle and hide under a thorn tree until it was time to wake up out of the trance and go home.

By the time I got to Maun, I was almost seven and my mother tried her usual trick of handing me over to the servants, but I was too old and experienced for that. Besides, I could manage without her now because I had the river. It was more constant than she, and I could walk down to its brown banks whenever I wanted and find it waiting for me. Every morning it was still there, beautiful and serene, and it always looked the same. At night, the moon would shine down, making the brown water turn silver as fish cut through the glass, splashing once, that single sound breaking the constant clatter of insects. The water kept on flowing, it knew where it was going, and it included me in its looped embrace; its slow sureness became the source of maternal comfort and peace. It became a sanctuary where my imagination caught fire, where the wind would speak through the thorn trees and I could hide from a world that was becoming increasingly terrifying.

Four

BY MAUN MY MOTHER WAS IN SERIOUS TROUBLE AND I
knew I wasn't going to be able to ditch her with the ease
that she'd ditched me in Swaziland. She was in her early
thirties, and she now fell into a depression that we were
both powerless to contain. I spent hours of my day hanging
around her door, or creeping close to her bed to press my
face up against the mosquito net rising and falling with the
slight breeze of the overhead fan. I stood and watched her,
staring in through the gauze as she lay on her bed with the
back of her hand on her forehead and her eyes closed.
Often she lay with her face turned to the wall. Her body
was locked against touch or communion, curled around as
if sheltering some empty space. She was terribly sad and
lonely, and all I could think was: What shall I do? What
shall I do?

Watching her lying there in her afternoon swoon, I

knew that she wasn't asleep; she was just pretending, just as she did at night. I felt that she did it so that she didn't have to get out of bed, walk down the corridor, and save me on those dark nights when the electricity generator stuttered into silence and the house lay down in darkness. Sometimes, in the early afternoon, when she lay under the mosquito net, I would lift it, timidly, ready to drop it at the slightest reaction. But of course there was no reaction because the game was that I wasn't there. She was quite safe: both of us knew that I wasn't going to be a nuisance or wake her. I was there because I had things to put down at the altar, next to the Bayer Aspirin bottle and the quinine tablets: a glass of water with a slice of lemon, or an orange cut into quarters; a painting of trees and blue sky, or a crayon drawing of a poinsettia I'd spent the morning doing. I had to stay and watch over her because I couldn't leave her alone that way.

After a while all I could do was to make myself as gone as she was. I sat with my back to the wall, crossed my legs, and waited and watched and made no sound or movement. I all but vanished into her reel of silence, into the numbing still heat of the darkened room. But at least I knew where she was and that was better than that time I'd come across her late one night, staring out at the blackness beyond the screen door, where the rain-filled wind was slapping the leaves of the banana tree. I called her name to make her turn and look at me, but then her thousand-yard stare was no longer directed at the night, but at me, and I couldn't take what I saw there in her eyes.

In the end, I'd have to leave her. I'd turn and go and before I knew it I'd find myself somehow back in the bush, running almost violently back to its fierce embrace. Out there in the blue emptiness nothing separated us but the thick, hot wind and, all around, littered in the sand, were diamonds scattered at my feet. If I waited under a tree for a long time, it was as if God came walking across the sand, strolling on the gold undulations that made waves under his feet. I had the wings of an egret and was borne up high, high, to gaze down at myself as I sat, stirring the dimple in the sand where the beetle hid from the sun.

Sometimes when I returned, something had happened, something had transformed her and the mother of the boat had returned, and for a little while all was forgiven. There's a fleeting memory of my mother, her hair bobbed with a Toni perm, leaning forward, elegantly bending from the waist in her full-skirted dress, her bare arms extended to take a bouquet from a little girl with bows at the end of her pigtails. She was smiling again, she was happy, everything was all right: she was the memsahib, the first lady of the bush, the District Commissioner's Wife. She was a representative of Her Majesty, Elizabeth II, the young Queen, crowned that same year, 1953, wearing the coronation crown and the golden robe, balancing the sceptre and orb in her small white hands. Out in the bush we were waving our flags and celebrating the new Queen as best we could, and it was all right again: glamour had touched my mother and brought her briefly back to life.

We went on picnics in the bush and we did it, I suppose, because the British love picnics, and so one didn't not have a picnic merely because the environment didn't lend itself particularly well to picnics. It was the same with meals: since that crowd was used to having a large meal at midday, with meat, potatoes and thick green vegetables, then that is what was cooked for them at each day's scalding point, and we ate it down to the last mouthful, leaving nothing on the plate, or else it would be served up, cold and coagulated, at the next meal. Spinach, which I simply could not swallow, was returned for days, with me just as stubbornly refusing it for days, until my mother would sigh and wave a hand at a servant, Oh, for God's sake, take it away. And then my ally and friend, Violet, would swoop in and whisk away the offensive slime and throw it to the dog, who didn't like spinach any more than I did.

One Sunday in December, we all went off to have a picnic by the side of a river on a boiling hot day. Rugs were laid out under the mopane trees, where the women sat with wicker baskets, fighting off the flies and ants, watching out for snakes and scorpions, and trying to keep the food cool as best they could. Boating was in the offing and we kids were excited. Hats were put on our heads. Nivea Cream was smeared on exposed flesh – sunscreen hadn't been invented yet. The white cream had an effect similar to that of continuously basting a chicken with butter. Soon our white flesh went scarlet, and when it began to hurt, we rubbed our shoulders with the cool rinds of watermelon and went back into the water to cool off, which increased the damage. It was a day for fishing, this was a crocodile-free zone, we were told, and a day for going out in the boat.

My father was steering the boat and we kids were carefully weighted around the sides; there were six or seven of us. Diesel fumes from the outboard motor filled the air. My father decided that the boat was too laden and someone got out. There was a fishing rod or two and off we went, heading for a small island in the middle. At some point, fairly far out, the small boat began to sink. The water was deep, we were a long way from help and none of us could swim except Angela, but she had somehow got a fishhook stuck in her toe. As the water began quickly to fill up the boat and the stern disappeared below the water, we all began to scream. In minutes we found ourselves flailing around in the water, mouths opening and closing on shrieks, brown water going over our heads, bobbing up and down in terror, certain we would drown.

My father managed somehow to keep us all afloat. He acted like a log on to which we hung for dear life and, though he couldn't reach the bottom, by extending his arms and letting us leech on to his shoulders and neck, he managed to keep afloat, and none of us drowned. He was Hercules with a litter of kids hanging on to his shoulders, and he kept us above water until another boat came roaring across to rescue us. It was a magnificent day, anointed by heroism. A day never to be forgotten: do you remember the day that Dad saved us all from drowning? And there were crocs in the water, too. And we nearly all died. Do you remember that day? And I could say to the others, who just had normal dads, it was my dad who saved us.

Bechuanaland was a landscape without boundaries and in it my father was back in a position of power. No one was looking over his shoulder, and certainly not my mother. He was given great liberty in a country where there were few restraints on white skin. He could do what he liked within his territory; he was lord of the bush, even as he was lord at home. He accepted no challenge to his authority and none was offered. He was given magisterial powers over a tiny community of whites and a vast community of blacks, who were pretty much unreachable in every way, except where the law touched them. Thus he could mete out harsh and unnatural punishment to a black man who'd stolen a white man's chickens, and turn a blind eye to the shooting of a white woman whose husband's gun went off one steamy afternoon while he was cleaning it close to her face.

There was power and excitement of a certain kind in the bush, at least for my father, but it was also a place of the most appalling tedium. Nothing to do. Nowhere to go. Only booze and sex, which took on perverse forms to try to make up for the slow ticking of the clock and the deadly inertia of days blurring into one another with nothing to show for it. Boredom of an excruciating kind could only be diverted by dangerous distractions. In our time, people went bush-crazy, or off their rockers. The most scandalous were those who went native – camouflaging themselves by merging with the landscape and the people in a useless attempt to escape its indifference. What they couldn't bear was that they had no effect, made no dent on the surface of a land that always returned to what it was. We would hear of people water-skiing in croc-infested rivers, or of some-one blowing his brains out after watching a beautiful sunset just one too many times.

My parents took no part in the debaucheries. They were high-minded and superior, strait-laced and aggressively proper: they didn't smoke and barely drank, and wouldn't dream of tossing their car keys into a hat to win a new sexual partner for the night. I don't know if they ever talked about what was going on when the sundowners and cocktail parties were over. With us, they pretended nothing was going on, and I was only aware of an underbelly, a dark, hidden side, when the body of a white man washed up on the banks of the river and the whispering began. He'd done the unthinkable by taking up with a black woman, and getting her pregnant, for which he'd been so ostracized that he'd drowned himself. Things like this, crossing the colour line, sexual matters, drove my father into a puritanical frenzy. He'd get red in the face and say how disgusting it was – sleeping with a wog, behaving like an animal, an Englishman not knowing how to behave.

He'd rant on and on, barely able to contain himself, getting more and more worked up: If that moron hadn't thrown himself in the river, I'd have done it for him. All I needed was a pair of clippers and I could have cleared up his problems all right. He'd blare this kind of thing all over the house, not bothering to hide his disgust from us, or the servants, or his tight-mouthed, repulsed wife. Hearing him this way was excruciating. I'd run out of the house and vomit into our beautifully manicured garden; I'd stand there retching and heaving, unable to understand why I was so upset and furious. Once, at the Victoria Falls, he was taking a photograph of the three of us, Angela, Susan and me. He had one knee on the ground and his other leg bent, trying to get us all in the shot. His testicles fell out of his shorts – he didn't wear underwear – and I stared in the utmost horror, frozen to the spot, my mind whirling in confusion and disgust when suddenly he yelled, Come on, say cheese, smile.

When we were little, we could hang out with the African children and play games in the backyard, but as we neared puberty, that all ended in a heartbeat. No one said, stop playing with the black kids – we just knew we had to go our separate ways, and so did they. Our childhood came to an end; we entered the white world and took on its prejudices and prohibitions. Our hearts closed and narrowed accordingly, and our minds became petty and afraid. It was different for the black kids; by that time they were too busy to play anyway. They were out hauling bundles of firewood, working in the fields, killing snakes, collecting water, carrying babies on their backs, or running along with a sibling dangling from a hip. The girls were taking deportment classes, learning how to balance an enamel bowl full of goat's milk on their head, or a bundle as wide as a cow, and the boys were out in the bush, getting cut.

My mother had always been uneasy about us spending too much time with the local kids. When asked, she wouldn't say why, but she became obsessed with disinfecting everything, getting the Dettol out at every turn in the day. If an African child had played with a toy, she'd boil it, or throw it out. She was endlessly complaining about the sores on their legs, which never seemed to heal, and the pus in their eyes and the white stuff around their mouths and little pointed penises. Their nakedness bothered her. The small boys often wore no more than a patch over their genitals, and the girls sometimes just a string of blue beads around their necks. The gobstopper belly button annoyed her. Why couldn't they cut the cord closer than that? Why did they have to make a mess of every single one? She could have provided a little basic medical attention herself, as some of the other Englishwomen did, but she didn't offer. Any door that might have opened for her, she shut; anything that might draw her out of herself and into the world around her, she turned her back on. Later, she would explain this by saying primly, but you see, dear, I never had to work, making it plain that, for her, a woman working was a sign of poverty, a lack of gentility. She said this all her life, not just in Africa. It was as if she was unable to understand that if not for her dependency, she could have got the hell out of there and escaped, with Angela and me tucked under each arm and Susan balanced on her head.

As she became increasingly lonely and unhappy, my father became increasingly distant, but perhaps it was the other way around. It's impossible to say. She had nothing to do but obsess about domestic matters – everything had to be spotless and white and she was harsh in the way she imposed her standards on the servants. My father was gone on his mysterious trips into the interior. When he wasn't exercising his powers as a magistrate, or dealing with native affairs, or overseeing a hanging, which was part of the job description, my father was deep in the swamps, checking out the tsetse fly. He took long expeditions out into the delta and the Okavango islands, the shady places where the tsetse fly loved to cool off, roosting in the trees, getting ready to take the blood of any wild or domestic animal, giving sleeping sickness to man and nagana to his cattle. The wildlife provided blood for the fly, but ironically, only man and his cattle were infected by disease – game never.

The first measures against the fly began in the forties: the idea was to deprive the fly of shade and blood and get rid of the problem that way. Trees were ring-barked where they stood, game was slaughtered wholesale, but of course only a limited area could be sacrificed in this way – a strip of land west of Maun, which kept us reasonably safe. Elsewhere, the tsetse flies flew off on their merry way, taking over the rest of the territory, which quickly surrendered to their dominion: the Africans moved out, the animals died, the grazing lands were deserted. It was a struggle the fly won hands down every time. Nowadays, aerial sprays keep them under control, where there's money for such luxuries, but in our day wherever the fly flew, man had to leave.

I once saw a man with sleeping sickness in our front room. Two women were walking him up and down, he was emaciated and shivering, and they dragged him around, trying to prevent him from falling into a sleep from which he'd never wake up. They talked loudly to him and kept smacking him and splashing water on his face, shaking him, urging him to stay alert. I don't remember if he lived or died, or why he was in our living room at all. The scene had a Victorian tint to it, which is why I'm sure I remember it. It seemed so un-African – the swoon-like state, the slipping over into death – it didn't make sense in a place where death came suddenly, brutally, and quite without melodrama.

Until the 1950s, Bechuanaland had been a land without fences. There were no barriers between one African's land and another's, and the wildlife roamed freely, coming and going as they chose, making their own seasons and giving the grasses time to replenish themselves. The Kalahari was famous for its golden grass and fat cattle. The grasslands lived in harmony with the migration patterns and a delicate balance was maintained. When the colonial government had taken over, it saw an opportunity and set up cattle-holding stations on the open grasslands, fattening up large herds before dispatching them to the abattoirs. In a couple of decades, the grassland had disappeared, thorn scrub replaced the golden perennials, dust storms gathered on the horizon, and the desert took over. By the end of the fifties, severe outbreaks of foot-and-mouth brought the cattle industry to a standstill. Cattle died like flies. The vets went out and shot animals and shoved them in deep mass graves, dumping lime over their dead bodies. Farmers went bankrupt in a day. You could smell the rotting. The cow had brought the grasslands to their knees and now foot-and-mouth was destroying the cow.

There was talk of bringing in the wire – an impenetrable line called the Kuki fence, which would divide the country into four quarantine areas to control the foot-and-mouth outbreaks. The wire went up and when it did, the free-roaming life of the Kalahari herds came to an end. The wire prevented movement from south to east, and it separated the herds of wildlife from water. British veterinarians cordoned off the land with a view to the government's priorities, which were to close the wires and to complete the fences as soon as possible. As a result, the elephant in royal procession, the buffalo and cantering impala, the troops of zebra and giraffe – all the great roaming herds making their way to water on ancient migration trails – galloped straight into the cordon fences and lay there till they died.

When we were in Maun, it seemed as though the abundance and the beauty of the wildlife would never end. You could see it best from a plane, looking down at a whole spilling network of game trails spread across delicate grasslands that have now turned to dust. Thousands, hundreds of thousands of wildebeest began to vanish in the mid-sixties when the grasses changed, causing the wildebeest first to thrive and then to become so plentiful that they were doomed to destroy their own food source and starve to death. The cattle brought in by the colonials took the rest of the grasslands, pushing out the wild herds of galloping antelope and gemsbok and zebra that had kept the grasslands going since time began.

These were the days when no roads crossed the vast unbroken savannah, where you followed the spoor on the sand and took your chances. When the Okavango was in flood and the water came gently down, the herds came with it, sniffing water in the wind, following the river's mysterious course to graze among the sedges, and to snort and cavort in the water. While rhino and springbok drank with bowed heads, lions sidled up seductively and struck, doing their job, keeping the vultures happy. Then, overnight it would seem, they'd all be gone, moving into the interior to find the shallow rainwater pans of the bushveld, endlessly moving back and forth over memory, tracing and retracing their footprints, returning to the places where they'd begun and where they would inevitably return.

Five

OUR TIME WAS UP, TOO. ONE DAY WE WERE TOLD THAT WE were leaving Maun. No explanation was given: we were being dispatched elsewhere and that was it. Orders from above, a new posting and a new home. A different district commissioner would take over my father's job, and he would be sent to where another white man was needed to fill a job almost identical to the one he'd just left. With little warning, we were packing up again and getting ready to leave. I don't know what my father felt about it. All I knew was that I was devastated: Maun would be gone, the desert and the delta would disappear and the river would be lost for ever. It felt that way – as if it would all sink without a trace when I was gone – but I knew really that it would go on without me and that once we'd left it would be as if we'd never been – as if my face had never been reflected in the speckled glass of the river, or as if Ange and I had never had tea parties up in the branches of the tree house, or seen the moon rise over the thorn trees and disappear into the clouds. In my heart I knew that the desert wouldn't miss me at all, and that when the wind blew, my footprint would vanish, leaving no memory of where I'd walked when my mind was adrift with loneliness.

Once we'd left Maun and the river – it was just the bush. We went from Maun to Francistown, which was a town, and something of a real one in that it was on the railway line, which ran right up to Rhodesia and all the way down to South Africa. It had some kind of school, certainly a few stores, a garage, a Barclays Bank, a cemetery, and perhaps even a hospital and a church. And not one, but two hotels: the Grand Hotel and the Tati Hotel, both on the main street. I think we spent some time when we first arrived in one of these hotels. There was a river, the Tati River, which flowed sluggishly into the Shashe River; and not far off was the Shashe Dam, so there was water at least, even if the river was usually dry.

I can see my mother quite distinctly in Francistown. I was, of course, still watching her like a hawk. Here, after a little flurry of anticipation, she was for a short time more at ease. She tried again with the garden and, since the soil was a little better, she had more success. She even managed to bring a lettuce to full term and presented it to my father with pride. He was pleased with it and he ate it with his dinner. But the dreariness of her life reduced her to inertia and pretty soon she was right back under the mosquito net every afternoon, curtains drawn, fan whirring and face to the wall. If I asked, hopefully, if she'd slept, she always said that she was just dozing. If I asked her if I could get her anything, she said nothing would help. By now she was plagued by neuralgia, a mysterious condition that she, or some physician, had named for her. It manifested as splitting headaches and dizzy spells – which could happen at any moment – and a tendency to faint, or to think that she would. Nothing could be done to relieve these symptoms, which went on for many years. If I spoke to her, she often ignored me, or made a mute shrug, or turned and walked away. Her silence was laden, full of a choked, impotent rage that had nowhere to go but into the racking headaches she now called neuralgia.

Many years later, back in civilization, still suffering, she went to numerous doctors trying to hunt down the source of the neuralgia, the dizzy spells, the passing out. The doctors came up with nothing. No doubt they thought her another hysteric. In the end, desperate for a condition to justify her suffering, she took up the suggestion that she should have her womb removed – this was at a time when doctors were gutting women's reproductive organs with enthusiastic regularity. She took a long time to recover from the operation, but it did give her, at last, an authentic reason to keep to her bed, and to ask of us quiet and consideration. Much, much later, the *petit mal* began and then the Alzheimer's, and throughout the long, lonely years, the depression was right there, the most faithful companion of her life, as was I, in my helpless fashion.

I would still keep my vigil on the other side of the mosquito net, but now once or twice I'd break through the pretence that she was sleeping. If she moved, I'd pull back the net and sit on the edge of her bed. Still she'd ignore me, but we both knew what she was up to. Once I waited a good long while, gathering up courage to ask her my question. I kept trying to speak and couldn't. Finally, she opened her eyes. What do you want? she asked, squinting through the glare, her hand to her forehead, palm up, fingers curled. I was just seeing if you needed something, I mumbled. What I need is beyond your comprehension, she said, turning her face away. I waited and waited. Then I just came straight out with it. Do you love me? She whipped round and looked at me as if I was some strange insect that had alighted on her bed. Don't be so silly, she snapped, and turned back to the wall.

After that, it took a couple of months to risk another topic of conversation. She'd not been able to reassure me that she had any feelings for me, and that somehow led me back to wondering about her own mother. Had she been loved? Was love, or the lack of it, behind all these problems we were having? She'd told us once that her mother was dead, and had died when my mother was nine. I was now nearing that age and in a place where other people had grandmothers, and I wanted to know about mine. I asked her about her mother, on a day when she was a little more cheery. She died, she said. But what was her name? Oh, didn't I tell you her name was Anne? No, I said, startled. Anne was my middle name. Well, she said, you were called after her. After a dead person? I was horrified. Nothing wrong with that, she said. I tried again. Where did she die? In India, of course. What did she die of? I don't know, she said, getting annoyed. I continued, in a way I knew she found irritating. What was she sick of, what did she die of? I don't know, she snapped, why should I know that? And then she took off. Why, she accused, are you always trying to find things out? Don't think I don't know what you get up to, how you go through the trunks on the stoep and prowl through my drawers and cupboards. You're always snooping, spying, asking questions. What's the matter with you? What are you looking for anyway? What are you trying to find out?

In Francistown, my father was going through a difficult patch. As a child, I had no idea what was eating him, but looking back on it, it seems pretty clear. Now that he was out of Maun, he was visible, and his actions had consequences. He was no longer way out there, lost in the interior. He was in a town of some structure where administrative forces could see what he was doing and could rein him in if he became over-zealous. The unbridled power of a man toughing it out against nature, obliterating anyone or anything that got in his way – those heady days had ended in Maun. By the time we got to Francistown, Tarzan had a boss. There was no more tramping through swamps, crocodile gun at the ready, and no more roaming the desert, armed against ticks and snakes, hunting out deadly insects or diseased cattle. In Maun, going to work had been pretty much like going on safari: every day my father went out into the bush with his natives, and each day he risked death in a fairly major way. His trips into the bush and the swamps were no orchestrated event: there was no cool tent and ironed sheets waiting, no good claret and venison laid out on a damask table under the flat-topped trees, with a safe view of the animals scheduled at six, with sundowners. When he returned from his trips in Maun, the house shuddered at his arrival. He'd storm the kitchen and toss a brace of dead ducks on the table, prop his guns on the rack, and kick his caked boots off on to a polished floor. He'd walk to his bedroom, throwing off his sweaty khakis as he demanded dinner and clean clothes. Master is home, the servants would whisper. We made ourselves scarce or, like the servants, snapped to attention.

My mother would be standing in some doorway, looking at the disorder of his arrival, at the red empty shells of his cartridges tossed next to her Spode teacup, at his burned face with the band of white where his hat shielded him from the sun. His knees, where the long shorts ended, would be scarlet, and his thick socks were covered in insects and blackjacks. He strode around, full of the ebullient, exhausted calm of a man who'd beaten back the darkness and come home to the Ice Queen. My mother would give him a disdainful glance and return to her chamber. Odd thing is, with all those snakes and crocs and all those diseases, I don't remember him ever getting sick, or bitten, or touched in any way by the violence of the environment, but my mother could finish him off in two seconds.

In Francistown, after lurking at the very back of my mind, almost out of sight, my father began to move into clearer focus for me. I can remember him quite clearly from this time, or at least his outside life is clear to me. He left the house early in the morning to go to an office, smartly decked out in pressed khakis and shiny shoes. A driver called Peter would collect him, standing smartly to attention beside the back door of the Chevy, holding it open, his hand touching his forehead in a brief salute. My father would step into it and be whisked away to do the things district commissioners did. My feeling is that he wasn't the only D.C. around, and that there were people he was rubbing up the wrong way. He was unable to take orders or to be a team player, and he took very poorly to authority. I was aware that he was struggling, and leaving the house in the morning, he was full of tension. I watched him, not the way I watched my mother, but I soon realized that I was watching him because I was beginning to plot against him, to find some way to overthrow him.

I remember his violence from this time, the physical side of it. In Francistown, his anger came out in a more terrifying manner than before. When he was around, we went on Red Alert and kept out of his way, padding about the house

73

like the servants, trying not to get on his nerves, or under his feet. His nerves were wired to his anger and could trip at any moment. Angela was more docile than I was and particularly dreaded the way he would shout and keep on shouting for hours. She kept out of his way entirely, whereas I skirted around him, ready to move if need be. If the houseboy forgot to polish his shoes, my father would kick him; if the cook made the soup too hot, he'd be bawled out. The back of my father's hand could knock a man sideways and he liked to do it. I took more of his physical and mental violence because I answered back. I liked to do it; it gave me satisfaction. Usually, if something – like a door whamming shut – annoyed him, he'd thrash out, but if he restrained himself for some reason, his face would set into its purple, lockjawed mode. He wouldn't be able to contain it for long and sooner or later he'd explode. His violence sometimes had a casual air. Once, while I was eating a mango, he strolled by and whammed the mango right out of my mouth, splitting my lip open.

Susan, still little, was not of interest to him in the way she was to become later, when, year by year, he came to fix upon her a deadly obsession that in the end made my mother superfluous. Susan at that time was big enough to be allowed to have close contact with her African nanny. Blond and curly-haired, she was enclosed in a triangle of soft blanket and travelled on a strong, black back, rocked back and forth as the nanny scrubbed the floor, or hung out the washing, or did the ironing. From where I stood, on the ground, it looked like the most heavenly place on earth and I longed to unseat her, but I was too big for all that. I'd come down to earth.

The parties and wild nights went on in Francistown and my mother could still come to life if her position in town demanded it. She'd be there to smile graciously and receive a bouquet from a child if the Queen's birthday was being celebrated, and she could put on a good dinner for a visiting dignitary. At night, she could wear her lovely dresses and go dancing on red polished stoeps that circled houses that were older and more gracious, but her high, false laugh was absent and there was desperation in her smile. We had a house there with a polished parquet floor softened with animal skins. The best was a lion skin with its head sticking up and its mouth open, revealing its snarling fangs and its beady black eyes. You could see the bullet holes by the fur that had rubbed off around them. But in spite of the skins, the kudu horns on the wall, the wooden masks and the African ornaments, it was an English room, the sanctuary and comfort of exiles, with furniture from department stores in London, flower prints on the wall, chintz-covered chairs and piles of out-of-date newspapers and magazines. These rooms perfectly reflected the British uneasiness with where they were – out in the middle of nowhere, miles and miles from home, never sure when their time would be up, or when the country would rear up and savage them.

There was more of a social life in Francistown, with

sundowners and garden parties, and Scandinavian visitors, who were fascinated by the Bushmen. New people passed through, stirring up the dusty life a little with their visits and gossip. There were things to do. Bulawayo was closer and we went to the Victoria Falls; we went several times, but it was never quite like the first time when the beauty and magnificence of those vertical rivers took my breath away. I was filled with awe, and a stunning sense of the sublime: we were in God's water palace and he was close at hand. Overlooking the Victoria Falls, carved on a statue of David Livingstone, was a line written by him: 'Scenes as lovely as these must have been gazed upon by angels in their flight.' I never forgot the line because to me it seemed to be all about Africa, or at least the part of it that I was clinging to for dear life. Because by now Africa had been cordoned off: one part contained the beauty, the other part was in darkness – a place far out of mind, where sudden images could flash, or ghosts could lurch and jump when I least expected to see them.

I fixed my eyes on the landscape and loved it with a passion that came close to religious ecstasy. Out there in the bush I could lose myself, vanish into the sand the way I'd once merged with the river: nothing could touch my soul, it was inviolate, and out there in the purging heat, my body would disappear too. This strange sense of dissolving couldn't have happened quite that way anywhere else on earth, or at least I don't think so. Out there in the African bush, in the middle of the day, in the utter and unearthly silence, there was something that made for visions. I think it was the air. It had a particular quality, impossible to describe, but it was as if the air was laced with mercury or lightning, or gin – it was liquid, rippling across the desert, leaving a stream of silver in its path. At midday the air hurt your eyes with its sharp intensity, and by two o'clock it was vibrating like a cobra's head. At this time of day, the air literally pulses; it changes the shape of things, pushing up the round hills, flattening the tops of the thorn trees, and smoothing out everything in between. But it can also suddenly rush up at you and make you feel slightly demented, and there are sparks in it that catch at your hair, pulling you this way and that. And while you're feeling this kind of derangement, you look up and there ahead of you is a giraffe with its head above a treetop, and it's as if both animal and tree have sailed up into the sky and are living there now. It's an African illusion, sometimes breathtaking and beautiful, but at other times frightening and unreal. There were days when I was jittery and afraid, out in the bush, and I'd see something moving up far ahead, a lone, black figure, eerie, almost supernatural. At first the figure appeared to be walking on air, but it was also not moving, and I got the curious sense that though the figure was walking straight at me, it would never reach me. In the same way, you could see a small blue hill up ahead and get the idea that you could reach it in a shot, but if you actually tried it, it would take you a day and a half.

These trips into the bush, where I saw things I couldn't

describe, or felt things for which there are no words, left me in a strange state. When I wandered back home, my mother would look at me as if I was a lunatic on the loose. I wore no shoes and the soles of my feet were tough and cracked. My face was burned red and I was often touched, either with sunstroke or by some strange, saving grace. Feverish and adrift, I would enter the house in a trancelike state. Go, she would say with her hand shaking, go and clean yourself up. You're filthy, you're covered in dust, and you smell like a native. You can't come to dinner looking like that. Take a bath, brush your hair, put on some shoes, get the calamine, and ask the girl to rub it on your shoulders. What a state! What's the matter with you? Why do you behave this way?

Angela was, I think, leading a more coherent life, but I can't seem to see it the way I could in Maun. I'm not sure who she was playing with, but I don't think it was me. I do know that at this time she began to side with my mother's irritation and confusion. She felt that I was making trouble, upsetting my mother, and causing my father to explode. She wanted me to just shut up and be more normal. She'd try to talk to me and tell me what I should do: just keep out of his way, don't answer back, and don't look at him as though you hate him, it just makes him crosser. I'd look away and off into the distance without answering her. Stop sulking, she'd say, come and have a swim. I'll teach you to play tennis if you want. I took up none of her suggestions. Okay, she'd say, but just make sure you keep away from Mummy.

Sometimes when I came in from the bush I did try to mingle with humankind for a while, but the whites bored me, and I found myself drawn to what was going on in the kraal where the Africans lived. Village life hadn't yet gone over to the shanty lifestyle that was to come later, specializing in houses made from planks and bits of corrugated iron, the roof held down with bricks, discarded crates serving as table and chairs and a hubcap for a cooking pot. Africans in the late fifties were still living in round, thatched huts formed in a circle, sheltered by a long mud wall decorated with red stripes and half-moons. They cooked in three-legged black pots; women squatted close to the fire, stirring water into the mealie pap and letting it cook till it was thick and dry, with a crust around the inside of the pot. They livened this up with wild rabbits and any meat they got from us, which was damn all, though there was plenty of it around. The children took out the cows and goats and brought them back at nightfall and the village was still living in an ancient rhythm that kept the rest of the world at bay.

Our servants, like our cook, Mpanda, who'd come from Nyasaland and never had enough money to return there to see his family, lived in a room at the bottom of the garden. There were several of these for the servants, and there was an outside latrine with a basin. The servants weren't allowed visitors in their rooms, but they sat under the trees, or outside the kitchen, with the servants from the houses across the way or down the street. The rooms were furnished with our discarded things, sagging beds with stained, striped mattresses, and chests of drawers that didn't close properly. Mpanda had a collection of my father's old clothes; they didn't fit him properly, so when he walked his trousers would flap in the wind. He had magazine photos on his wall of his pin-up girl, Elizabeth II, the young Queen, and this, along with his Bible, was his most precious possession. We had to keep away from their quarters and when I went down, to ask Mpanda to help me make a slingshot, or to fix a puncture, I was breaking the rules.

We were becoming vaguely aware of cracks in the rigidly maintained colonial structure as the winds of change began howling through Africa. In Ghana, the British had changed the constitution for Nkrumah in 1951. He'd been elected while in jail for sedition and the British had released him and made him premier, giving the colony broader powers of self-government. Everyone loved Nkrumah because he knew how to think white – he'd learned some British tricks that enabled him to hold on to power and to create some stability in West Africa. It was the beginning of self-government in the colonies and people were already saying that soon it would be our turn to hand over the keys. The natives were developing an attitude, and people were starting to lock their doors and buy more guns. Girls were being taught to shoot. Later on came the white-house-as-armed-fortress, with security fence and electric gate. This all began with the Rhodesian

Civil War, when Ian Smith and his crowd wouldn't go for majority rule and declared the colony independent. The security business spread over into South Africa, where business got brisker every day.

Back in the B.P., the blacks knew we were getting edgy and they loved it: they could push things, cop an attitude, do less, and get away with more. And once the rigidity went out of the structure, it began to collapse. You could feel it in the wind, and at night when the light gave the distance a new shape, the small hills darkened and the moon came through the clouds like a fang. We felt it running through the mealie fields playing war games: once we'd run off screaming that the Germans were coming; now we were imagining blacks coming after us with machetes and Russian rifles. The blacks knew what we were thinking. They'd always known and they were way ahead of us, biding their time.

Beyond the neat streets of Francistown, where the whites were getting drunk and making fools of themselves, was the hidden, dark side of life. I was of course not supposed to go anywhere near it. It was particularly dangerous to creep too close to the kraal after nightfall. From my bed, I could hear the singing on feast nights and the volley of the drums, and I was drawn there when parties were going on and I knew I'd not be missed. I would creep over to the kraal, hiding behind a hut to watch the dancing around the fire. Sour, fermented beer was handed around in gourds or jam tins and the dancing went wild. Some nights the witch doctor would come and I'd watch in fascination as he hummed and chanted, huddled over his bones and blood, and wait for that moment when he'd have a fit and pitch over in the dirt, sticking his tongue in the sand. I never knew what he was summoning up – rain or blood, fat cattle, or the hide of the white man.

The feast days intimidated the whites. There was a suspicion that even the good Africans – those cleaning our floors and living at the bottom of our gardens – were being stirred up by the independence fervour coming from West and Central Africa. A nationalist virus was spreading fast throughout the continent and the Europeans were trying to prepare for it. In Bechuanaland, though, it still felt far off in the hills and beyond the dark rivers, over the borders and far away. The British were relying on a continuation of the long drift of peace that had marked Bechuanaland's slow, steady progress. There seemed no reason why we should give up our overseas possessions: why pull out when it would all go to pot without us? Whenever a passing thought surfaced about what right do we have to be here, it was instantly countered by the imperial notion of what right do we have to leave? We had Seretse Khama, after all, and he'd been educated in England, and was married to Ruth, a white woman. He had children of a nicer shade and was practically an aristocrat. He was the big chief, the black man in charge. He could be allowed into the house for a whisky and soda. We'd be okay.

In actual fact, we were more afraid of polio than independence. I certainly was. Polio and snakes were the terrors of my life. A neighbour of ours, who made delicious sponge cakes, looked up one afternoon and saw her small son bitten by a green mamba. She'd watched the whole thing happen: working out in her garden, pruning, she'd looked up to see a beautiful emerald body, a shimmering rope that seemed to be part of the bougainvillaea tree and inseparable from its foliage, uncoiling and unwrapping its length, moving slowly, until it stopped and transfixed her with its black eye. Then its awful, primordial head took aim and flew straight as a pole at her boy, who was running a car along in the pale dirt, unaware of the soft blue cave of the mouth opening, coming right at him. The two fangs pierced his leg. In the second it took for his mother to reach him, his face was white and draining, his mouth a scream of death. She ripped off the belt of her shirtwaist dress, made a tourniquet around the top of the boy's thigh, and then pressed her lips over the two neat fang-holes and sucked the poison out, sucking and spitting before carrying the boy to the snakebite kit, which, by itself, wouldn't have been of any earthly use by then. I remember how we looked at him afterwards, walking around, right as rain. And how I looked at her, a mother who'd been there to save her child from dying.

So many times there were these near-death experiences with snakes: the cool coil in the bathtub, the black mamba perfectly matching the black beneath your bed, the twenty-foot python with the bulge of a pullet in his belly, saving it for later. Or, how about trying to kill the snake: hacking at its throat, chopping it up with a kind of joy, running it over with a jeep, back and forth, feeling that hideous speed-bump roll. Was it dead yet? Could you ever kill it? It'd come back in your dreams for weeks, making your flesh crawl whenever you heard that one was hanging around someone's back door, or had taken up residence in a henhouse up the road. There was the little boy climbing the mango tree, who put his hand on a mamba, thinking it a branch wet with rain. And the jealous husband who trapped a puff adder in the cooking pot and left it for his wife to come back to from the fields. I almost sat on a snake sliding down a sandy slope in our back garden. The snake put its head out to look around on a hot, hot day and my sister grabbed hold of my legs, skinning my thighs and wrenching me to safety. To this day, I cannot see a hose left out on the lawn at night without fearing for my life.

Polio seemed worse, far worse, than any of these: one morning you could wake and you'd got it; the test was: can you touch your chin to your chest? If you couldn't, you had polio. Your life was over, and you could also kill your entire family. It was the plague, the epidemic of then. In America, if there was an outbreak of polio, they closed the beaches and no one went into the water. In Africa, there was no such thing as an outbreak; polio was always there, carried by the sewage that floats in every pond and river. Polio enters your body orally and infects the intestinal lining: it goes straight to the bloodstream and into the central nervous system. Overnight you become crooked and crippled, or can't breathe. You're deformed, blind, have limbs amputated, or you're just plain dead. You drown in your own secretions or get put in an iron lung, where your body is enclosed in a narrow pressure chamber that breathes for you. Only your head is sticking out: it's a breathing coffin that you have to stay in all the time, buried alive. Kenya had a few iron lungs, but we had none, and barely a hospital to put one in. After 1956, the Salk vaccine reached us in the bush, and we, being white, were vaccinated. But that was too late for many of the children, whose lives were over by then, one way or the other.

I remember being so terrified of getting polio that all water became contaminated, every pond, every river, every swimming pool and bathtub. It's hard to describe the enormous sense of terror associated with that word. It was so easy to catch. Babies got it and were gone in a heartbeat. Death was close in our world in so many ways and yet the iron lung was more horrible than death. By seven, according to the Jesuits, children have arrived at the age of reason and can contemplate death. By then, the idea of death was fully imagined in my mind, and not just any old death – mine. I was morbidly afraid of the dark. I'd had a number of accidents where I'd nearly drowned. Suffocation terrified me beyond all else, and polio presented the nightmare in its most vivid form. I knew what suffocation felt like. I started having nightmares again, the way I had in

Swaziland when I was six. I woke sitting bolt upright, heart beating wildly, mouth parched, gasping for breath. I'd dreamed that someone had put a pillow over my face and held it there, and just when I thought I was going to die, I blacked out. The dream repeated, becoming more and more vivid, and when the morning came, I often thought it must really have happened, but how could that be when I was still alive?

I began to think more and more about my grandmother, Anne. Why didn't my mother know what she'd died of? If my mother was only nine, her mother couldn't have been old, and old was the only good reason for a person to die. Did my mother have what her mother had had? And in that case, did I have it too, and not know it the way my mother didn't seem to know what her mother had? Did Angela have it? And Susan? Were we all doomed to die of this mysterious disease? If it were typhus or T.B. surely she would have said. Snakes and polio were manifestations of death in my imagination, but insidiously something else began to be just as frightening – the idea of madness. My mother looked at me at times as if she thought I was mad. I too thought I was mad when my mind seemed to split in two and I couldn't find part of it, or when I couldn't remember where I'd been for hours on end, or on those mornings when I'd wake up and my bed wasn't the way it had been when I'd got into it, and it looked as though I'd been thrashing about all night like a lunatic.

I attached myself like a leech to one of our servants,

Elizabeth, who was particularly kind and motherly, and I forced Angela to take care of me. A helpless dependence came over me all of a sudden, and I was no longer the bushchild, the explorer, the spy in the African camp. Angela took me under her wing; she was tough with me but she allowed me to be her friend. She didn't want to look after me, she made that clear, but she felt she had to. We were conspirators in a silence, and it bound us together in a way that infuriated her, but from which she couldn't escape. Perhaps she was afraid that already I was like my mother, a bag of nerves and a basket case.

I took up a similar role with Susan, taking care of her when I didn't want to. She was a sweet child, but also a pain in the neck, a tag-along shadow that I wanted to push into the bushes. I had to watch out for her: she was little sister, vulnerable as an egg, and I knew the ropes by then, the way I knew the backyard. It was up to me to protect her. But for as long as Angela was around, I didn't spend too much time on this watch. We two, being so much older and with only two years to divide us, tried to go our own way and left Susan to nannies as much as we could. I was too busy trying to hang around Angela to keep looking over my shoulder for Susan. Soon, Angela would be off to boarding school and then everything would be lonelier.

Meanwhile, Angela was giving me tips that were to last a lifetime. She taught me how to make perfect scrambled eggs and Marmite soup on the highly inflammable child's stove that I treasured. We played with this paraffin stove for hours in the back, folding parsley, which blossomed abundantly under a dripping tap, into the glossy eggs. We ate our scrambled eggs, legs spread out in front of us, sitting under the lemon trees. Angela learned how to make a mean lemon meringue pie, crunching Marie biscuits for the base and stirring lemon rind into the thick, shiny lemon custard. She used the real stove for this and showed me how not to burn myself, and what to do if I did. She'd already taken up her station as nurse and would return to it again and again throughout her life.

Those long, hot days of play, the last days when we were always together, day and night, seem not to have lasted that long. They fit into a small frame that extended from Maun through some of the time in Francistown and ended when we reached Gaberones. We walked and ran bare-legged under the citrus trees and made houses between the roots of the frangipani trees, ran down to the river and spent hours high up in the tree house, watching the river. I think of her thick, dark brown hair bobbing ahead of me. She was a beautiful child, smiling but pensive. Often she seemed, in memory, to have been with someone else, but perhaps that was just in Maun, with Barbara Riley. I have a sense of hanging around on the edges of her friendships, watchful of her, as she was watchful of me. I seem to see her head turning backward, her eyes glancing nervously over her shoulder, to see if I was all right, if I could make it on my own without her.

Our sisterly bond was kept loose, mainly because our

parents wanted it that way, setting us up against each other, the better to control us. A deeper alliance came later, when we each had a daughter of our own, born within a month of each other. As Ally and Amanda grew up, we went away together, on weekends and holidays, with our husbands and daughters, or had dinners together, or took tea in our tiny gardens in London. We always achieved an easy, flowing connection in the kitchens of our lives. A strong, sisterly sense returned around a stove and, just as in our childhood hours, we would stir and move around each other effortlessly, handing a knife, or moving to the task most in need of completion, without words, having the habit of cooking and the making of meals to remind us of who we were and where we'd come from.

Angela became independent from an early age, but hers wasn't the kind that grew out of a mother's nurture. There wasn't, and didn't ever come to be, a natural and close connection between our mother and Angela. Angela remembers reaching a point where she set our mother aside. It happened in Gaberones. Angela was eleven, away at boarding school, when someone, unexpectedly, gave her a ride home. She was standing at the gate, all excited to be home, and she went into our house only to have our mother say curtly: Why are you here? A sense of being an inconvenience, a nuisance, overcame and crushed Angela, and it was then that she gave up on our mother, and went her own way.

Angela was my keeper while she was at home and later

she was put in charge of me when I joined her at the boarding school in Johannesburg. It was a tough job. The caretaking had started in Swaziland, just before we'd been sent to Goedgegun, when, late at night, she'd come across to my side of the room when I was crying and tell me to go back to sleep. What was it like sleeping in the same room, we two, our small beds pressed against opposite walls as we heard each other sleep and breathe, or caught a muffled cry when a nightmare broke the surface of the night? What was she dreaming in that deep still that came down over the house when the electricity generator stuttered out and the house fell into darkness? And, when moonlight crept through the window, crossed the floor and climbed up over the bright, white covers of our beds, illuminating our life as sisters, was Angela, like our mother and me, also pretending to be asleep?

Six

AFTER A BRIEF SPELL IN FRANCISTOWN, WE WERE SENT OFF
to the capital of the B.P., and here, in Gaberones, my mother
was able to recover herself a little. In the first place, my
father was more important; he was district commissioner of
the biggest town in the B.P., and since Gabs was a step up
for him, my mother felt it increased her importance as well.
Gabs at the time was just a scruffy town with some
additional administrative buildings: a courthouse, a jail, a
hospital, a school and a police station, plus more stores and
roads, more houses and more farms on its outskirts. It had
some older houses with well-established gardens, with tall
oleander bushes around the walls and beautiful flame trees
with flat tops that made pools of shade for cats and dogs. In
Gabs, at least, visiting predators wouldn't pick off our pets.
Lettuce could survive in Gabs, and in fact we had a very
good garden, with Cape gooseberries, hard little peaches,

peas, beans, white potatoes and fat tomatoes, along with the usual mangoes, citrus, corn, pumpkins and sweet potatoes. My mother grew some flowers and she even managed to get a rose bush to flourish, and there was a sprawling grapevine with tight bunches of fragrant grapes that made black triangles among the green. Sometimes a snake would catch your eye, peering out between the leaves, not venturing out until the sun had set.

I think that the garden, and the traces of normality, and also our removal from a life that had felt utterly barbaric, helped my mother to settle at Gabs. We stayed here for a couple of years, which was a long stretch for us, and it must have been comforting to her. We lived in a nice house with a flagpole in the garden and, whenever we got a chance, the Union Jack was up there, waving in the breeze. In Gabs my mother rallied sufficiently to teach Mpanda how to make babootie pie, which is a kind of curried shepherd's pie, and mulligatawny soup. She ordered spices and pappadoms from the Republic and began to make her own curries, using local mutton and chickens, and trying her hand at parathas and nans. She bottled lime and mango chutneys, and in this way a little of her life in India came back to her and made Africa more palatable.

In Gabs we could even go to the movies. You sat outside watching a rickety screen under the trees, or in a room in the hotel, where someone shouted Lights whenever something went wrong. We watched *Pathé News* followed by a scratched-up version of *Seven Brides for Seven Brothers*, or something even more out-of-date – we got movies years and years after they'd run in America. Usually the projector broke down a few times and it took ages to fix and we all got restless waiting for that strange underwater sound to bubble up as the projector swam back to life and the reel started to roll once more. The circus also came one time, Boswell's, I think it was, complete with tent, sawdust, people flying through the air, and candy-floss. It was extraordinary to see lions and elephants that way in Africa – all of them neatly trained, with just a whip to keep them in line. The elephants sat politely on stools waving their arms in the air, the lions roared for effect and not for blood, and jumped through hoops rather than ripping out an impala's throat or eating a child in front of its parents.

I went to a school with a teacher called Miss Klopper. She was a large, sweaty Afrikaans woman who lived next door to the school, in a house where she took in two small boys, orphaned by distance, or by family trouble, to her kindly care. I remember learning how to make my writing very neat and round, using a ballpoint pen for the first time. I also learned a little arithmetic and some South African history: Miss Klopper was very keen on the details of the Great Trek, and devoted to the patriot Paul Kruger, and she had a particular fondness for the battles where the Boers had licked the Brits. She taught me some Afrikaans and I liked it this time, and I remember a poem in that language; it was about murder: 'Bloed in die water en bloed in die laan, wie is dit wat daar so geruisloos gaan?'

On Valentine's Day I drew a card for Dawie Swart, the boy who had family trouble, and he in turn gave me my first bouquet. Of course we all knew what the family trouble was – mother a lunatic, father living with a black woman – but no one said a word. As for Dawie, whatever his family gave him brought on some kind of catatonia; he would sit, mute and frozen, beyond reach or reason, and, as with my mother, I could do nothing for him.

Angela had gone to boarding school again, this time to a convent in Mafeking that was later to expel her. I was lost without her, but it also gave me a chance, like my mother, to recover myself a bit too. I had a room to myself, with a red-tiled stoep beyond it; on this stoep was a tin chest that had travelled from India to England and then on to Africa. In it was my mother's satin wedding gown. It had yellowed like a complexion and was wrapped carefully in muslin with a small box of love letters tucked in at the waist. I'd been through the contents of all these trunks and chests – on the scent of anything that might lead to some under-standing of our strange family. In one of these chests, I found a picture of my namesake, my grandmother, Anne Webb, and I kept it for a day or two until I knew her face by heart. When I covered her eyes with my hand the rest of her looked uncannily like my mother. She also seemed to be very miserable and quite without vitality. After studying her face, I tried to smile a lot, as if this way I could some-how manage to escape the family malady, whatever it was.

My mother picked up the maternal role a bit more in

Gabs, and as a result I got overly attached to her again. She did wonderful birthday parties for us there, and since there were more kids around, the presents were more plentiful and better in quality. I gave my mother some of the presents I got for my birthdays – things like manicure sets and bubble bath – things I knew she'd like. I always sort of wished she'd give them back. I hoped she'd say, you keep this, dear, it's yours. She didn't. We wore party hats and there were streamers and balloons. Mpanda made beautiful cakes, and little English sandwiches, with the crusts cut off. There were sausage rolls in flaky pastry, Cadbury's chocolate fingers and potato crisps. In Gabs, every kid in town came to these parties, and so the servants were all enlisted in cutting oranges in half, leaving a handle of rind, so that it looked like an orange basket. When the pulp and pith were scooped out, they'd be filled with scarlet jelly. These were greatly admired.

My mother's contentment was brief. There wasn't enough to sustain it, and before I knew it she had vanished behind the net again, squandering her days in sleep, and keeping up a regular supply of headaches to justify her absence. I watched her go down, and before long I, too, was as low as a snake in a well. There was less to keep me alive in Gabs because there was nothing in the way of beauty: it was just an ugly little dorp squatting on the main road and railway line, close to the border of the Republic. I should, of course, have been making friends by now, but it wasn't happening. I was as lonely as ever – unable to trust connection and unwilling to risk affection, keeping away from people, afraid they'd find out something about me if I let them get too close.

I remember being aware of sex by Gaberones and it horrified me to know that every adult I'd heard of had been up to it, including the Queen. The African women had children by several different men: the men went off to the mines and the women brought up the children with the help of their mothers and sisters. It seemed a good way to me – a houseful of children, each having a different father and one who didn't stay too long. My mother gave me a book about the facts of life; actually it was about chickens and their reproductive cycle – close enough to do the trick, I suppose. The subject wasn't mentioned again. I had a deep revulsion against sex by then and I didn't want it ever brought to my attention. I couldn't think about it and when kids started to talk about it, I left immediately.

A pack of boys, many of whom were from the same family, were beginning to flaunt their sexuality. The Cawoods made up a tribe, eleven children in all, and not even the excuse of being Catholic to account for such a total. Several of the Cawoods must have witnessed the primal scene because they certainly knew what they were doing. They, and a few other boys, took some girls up to the flat rocks where the little turtles swam in the rain pools, and began fooling around. The flat rocks were a place I liked to go and I saw them there in their happy nakedness and, distraught and disgusted, I rode my bike home at breakneck speed. I was frantic to tell my mother, to reveal to her what was going on. As soon as I got home, I threw the bike in the dirt at the back door and raced in to find her. She was reading a magazine in the drawing-room and was dismayed to see me. What on earth's the matter with you? she said, raising a hand as if to ward off an attack. What are you so worked up about? And don't get so close to me, you're sweating and covered with dust. She pulled herself back into her chair, and as I threw my confession at her, I watched her face recoil. She didn't want to hear, she wanted no details, and she shut me up as fast as she could. I don't want you to talk about this again, she said. Do you hear? Not another word. She went back to her magazine, but her coldness couldn't touch me. I was jubilant. I'd broken a silence and exposed a crime. I'd told. As I was leaving the room, I turned to look back at her and saw that she was looking at me. A strange ripple passed between us, guilty, almost collusive, and then she looked away in a flash and so did I.

She passed the information on to my father. He didn't ask me about it, didn't even try to verify the incident with me, or accuse me of making it up or lying, which was what I'd expected. Instead he went ballistic and stormed the Cawood house, where he attacked Mr Cawood with such moral fury that the whole town was left reeling. He said not a word to me, ever. But the incident ruined any chance of a friendship in that town for me. I was a louse and a scab, and no one would have anything to do with me after that.

But then there was Mally. She came from a one-horse

town called Molepolole and she lived with us for six months so that she could go to Miss Klopper's school. I was very glad to have her. Her presence in my bedroom at night provided safety and comfort and we would whisper together when the electricity shut off at eleven o'clock. While Mally was in my room I had no nightmares. I noticed that my father treated Mally in a different way from the way he did me – perhaps because she was not given to moods and rages; she was instead a blond, plump girl with hard, dimpled cheeks and a round chin and sweet nature. She giggled a lot. My father began to play a game with Mally that took place every night after we'd had our bath together and put on our nightclothes. She had a nightgown with small slits down the sides. During her time with us, these slits got longer and longer because my father would chase her down the long corridor in the Gabs house and her nightie would split as she ran. She would be shrieking and giggling at the same time as the slits in the nightgown extended higher up her thighs until it was pretty much ripped in two. He would be chasing and snatching at her with a fatuous leer on his face. I would stare at him with incomprehension: who was this man in relation to my cold-blooded father? Who was he when he did these things? I tried to convince myself that he had nothing to do with me – that we weren't really related at all.

Once Mally had gone, our house returned to its old routine. I was alone in my bedroom at night, and my fear of the dark became so chronic that I was allowed my nightlight again. I developed insomnia and, when I did manage to fall asleep, I had nightmares – the same old nightmares, a disembodied hand holding a pillow over my face, or trying to kill me with a knife, faces looking through my window and hands running up and down the window panes. I started sleepwalking and sometimes woke to find myself curled up on the floor in the spare room, or hidden behind the chair in the drawing-room, close to the curtains. I was fast becoming a wreck, babbling the Child's Prayer to myself every night, thinking I wouldn't make it to morning.

I was eleven going on twelve when I became fully aware of my hatred for my father. The intensity of it helped me to shove aside some of the terror I felt in his presence. But knowing how much I hated him left me twitchy, constantly jumping out of my own skin, and weird as can be. I kept having flashes of sticking a knife into him, or of shooting him, and it left me feeling crazy. I didn't understand why I felt the way I did, but I couldn't control it at all, and soon it seemed to be controlling me.

My father had a way, when I was involved in my homework, or when my mind was off roaming, of creeping up behind me to suddenly twist my ear, or flick it hard with his thumb and forefinger. When I spun round, wanting to break his face open, he'd laugh and stroll out of the room. He did something similar with my dog, Jasper, who was a small but feisty black-and-white Scottish terrier, who loved to bay at the moon. Sometimes, of an afternoon, my father's eye would light upon my dog and he would lift him up by his front paws, speak to him in a queer kind of doggy language, and then hurl him down on to his back with great force. He'd watch Jasper lying there at his feet, howling and winded – as helpless and humiliated as a beetle, and would stroll off, a vacant look on his face.

At night, when I lay sleepless in the dark, I began to plan my father's death. There were two possible weapons: the double-bore elephant gun, which would make a real mess, or the kitchen knife. The murder fantasy grew stronger and pretty soon it entered the light of day. I found myself thinking about it when we were all sitting around the dining-room table, eating huge meals in the sweltering noonday heat. My father ate very fast, shovelling food into his mouth without tasting it. His way of eating was barbaric and brutal. When he'd finished, he'd toss his starched, ironed white napkin right on to the dirty plate and leave the table. It was then that I wanted to get him, but something told me that I wasn't ready to do it yet. I wasn't brave enough to kill him yet, but in the meantime I put myself behind glass walls, and pretty soon I got to be so checked out that I didn't see him, or even hear him, when he spoke. I got so good at blanking him out that one evening I didn't hear him when we were seated in the dining-room, waiting for dinner to be served.

My parents always dressed for dinner; they came to the table fresh and fragrant for the ritual of dining, and took up positions at either end, facing one another, separated by an armoury of cutlery, polished silver and crystal. I was in the middle, sitting in silence, but in a real way I wasn't there at all. So I jumped when my father's voice, loud and angry, finally reached me. I looked at him dully, not having heard what he'd said. I came to and heard him snap, Go to your room and try to find something to wear that makes you look less of a freak. The air stiffened. My mother said, Hurry up, dear, go on now. Don't keep dinner waiting. There were only the three of us for dinner in those days: Angela was away at school and Susan was fed earlier in the kitchen. He began to yell: Look at me when I'm speaking to you, you stupid cow. I didn't move; I barely breathed. His fist landed on the table, which jumped. My mother jumped. She began to dab at her mouth with her napkin, and the scarlet of her lipstick flared off the white linen. I kept my eyes fixed on the napkin as she let it flutter to the table like a gesture of surrender.

He was up on his feet, bawling me out, and in a second his thumb and second finger clamped on my jaw and twisted my head in his direction. I told you to look at me when I'm speaking to you. My mother began to cower in her chair, whispering ... The servants ... must you? ... Can't we just have dinner in peace? From my pinned position, I stared him down, and continued to do so until he'd knocked me sideways and on to the floor.

I was still too scared to go after him directly, too afraid that he might kill me first, so instead I began to torment my little sister. I was twelve, which meant that Susan was six – my age in Swaziland exactly – and perhaps it was because of this, seeing her at the same age as I'd been when my life crashed, that some madness came over me. I'd been playing with her in a normal enough way up to then: pushing her on the swing, teaching her how to pump with her legs, showing her how to make houses the way Angela and I had done under the trees, even lowering myself to make mud pies with her. Slowly the games changed. At first I just teased her, but it got so bad that I made her cry, and soon she was wailing for me to let her go back into the house to find Elizabeth. I wouldn't let her. I took her instead out into a small cluster of orange trees and I made her take off all her clothes. When she cried, or tried to refuse, I hit her. She annoyed me by picking up a handful of dirt and chucking it in my face. It got into my eyes and I nearly lost it: I could see myself stuffing dirt into her mouth until she suffocated, but the vision in my head so terrified me that I stopped. Something else occurred to me. It came as a fully formed image and I couldn't get it out of my mind. I found myself picking up a stick. See this, I said in a Scottish accent, I'm going to ram this right up between your legs till it comes out your gob. She looked up at me, her face swollen, her mouth ajar, and the terror in her eyes hit me like icy water. I came to. I was bewildered. I didn't know who I was – was this person with the Scottish accent me? Or was there another me? Or was that a mad girl who was somehow wearing my clothes? I helped Susan to dress, and cleaned her face. I didn't have to tell her not to rat on me. She knew better by then. All I knew was that I was in serious trouble, and that if something or someone didn't save me, I might kill someone.

Seven

LEAVING GABERONES ON THE MAIN ROAD AND HEADING
south, you come to two white arched walls with a cattle
grid between them, and a sign that says Bonnington. Up
ahead stretches a long dirt road that takes you up to an
L-shaped house. On your right, tall silos rise like spires to
gaze over a parched and desolate landscape. The silos waft
out strange and pungent odours: sour beer and yeast with a
dash of fermenting flowers. In pens close to the silos the
pigs grunt and forage. An oblong of green grass stretches
out in front of the house, halted abruptly at one end by a
low wall covered in bougainvillaea, and at the other by
a narrow veranda that runs the length of the house. The
sprinklers are on, and there are a few deep dents in the
lawn where a naked foot has moved the sprinklers to new
locations. Brown and gold tortoises amble through flower
beds stuffed with nasturtiums, daisies, scarlet geraniums

and a few blue agapanthus. In the distance are the mulberry trees and a tennis court, and way beyond those the lands take off, connected by long, winding tracks.

If you walk for a bit back there, you'll come across a brown-watered dam with an island of trees in the middle where wild birds roost. Small boys, clutching their knees to their chests, bang into the water off the rocks, or trail sticks in the sand under the willows that straddle the dam. Close by is a large kraal enclosed by fences of thorn bushes to keep the livestock in and the hyenas out. Inside these walls, which roll away in a sand storm, a straggling village of thatched huts and brick structures provide for human habitation. The women are stamping the mealies under the thorn trees and drinking hot sweet tea while their babies sleep on their backs. A boy plays a penny whistle and shuffles his feet in the sand. Dung beetles shove huge cargoes in front of their faces, moving fearlessly between the hooves of goats. Hens scratch at the cracked earth as if there's something to find, and roosters crow all day.

This is the le Cordeur farm, or this is how it was when I was there. It wasn't a long drive from Gabs, but when you got there everything felt wilder and drier. Once you left the little British enclave with its streets and subdued gardens, you were right back in the bush and the le Cordeur farm was an oasis in the middle of it. It was another Maun, but without the river. Every morning the sun shot into the sky and hung there threateningly, the sand dragged on for ever, the insects gave out their insistent lament, and there was no breath of air. Droughts came frequently, and water had to be stored in reservoirs and tanks and used sparingly. If the rains came, overnight the earth was covered with wild-flowers, and we all went nuts, black and white, screaming with joy, whooping it up, catching raindrops on our tongues. When there was thunder, the Africans bolted under the beds and hid there until it had passed and, if you were indoors, you'd listen to the racket of the rain hitting the corrugated-iron roof so hard that it was as if a drunk was stumbling about up there over your head.

And to think that we might never have reached the farm had Angela not been having such trouble at Mafeking Convent. The nuns there were giving her a hard time. They couldn't understand how an Irish and Catholic girl could actually be refusing to have anything to do with the Catholic Church. Angela was resisting all urgings towards mass, confession and confirmation, and the nuns were determined to break her and pull her back into the fold. They bullied and intimidated her, threatened her with hell fires and purgatory, and dropped rosaries on her as she slept at night. Nothing would persuade Angela to change her mind: she set her will against theirs and refused to budge. My mother was furious with her and my father was sympathetic, but it wasn't looking good. It seemed pretty certain that she'd be kicked out of the convent.

I think this problem with Angela and the convent was what began the friendship between our parents and the le Cordeurs – who knew of a good boarding school in

Johannesburg. There would have been no other reason for the friendship. The le Cordeurs were not my parents' kind of people – not one of Us, my mother said firmly. They were farmers, the descendants of Huguenots who'd trekked inland from the Cape in the seventeenth century to get away from the British. These early Huguenots had intermarried with the Dutch settlers and moved into the belly of southern Africa, setting up homesteads and churches in a land they loved fiercely. To be so at home in Africa was a notion astonishing to the British, so, to my mother and father, the le Cordeurs and their kind were a mystery, and one not to be explored.

Immediately after we'd made our first visit to the farm, my mother, who'd taken one quick look into what she called the drawing-room, sniffed and turned up her nose. Very Dutch, she said, but she was more than happy to leave us with the le Cordeurs for a few months while she and my father sailed Home with Susan on a Union-Castle boat. We stayed on the farm over the summer holidays more than once, but it was the first time that changed my life. The minute I took my suitcase out of the car and watched my parents drive away, with a bunch of mangy, snarling dogs seeing them off, I knew I'd reached sanctuary. Rena le Cordeur hugged and kissed us. Angela immediately took off with Myfanwy, who was about fifteen, and I was left with Rena. She led me into the house by the hand. It was all I needed: if I could have, I'd have curled up in her lap then and there and not budged for the duration.

She led me into a dark, cool room with heavy chairs and curtains, and a piano. Everything about the room had a certain kind of gravity. It was a little airless, the curtains keeping out most of the sun and light, and there were wool rugs on the floor. It smelled of beeswax. The furniture was unfamiliar. There were no chintz-covered chairs and Queen Anne tables; there were no mounted animals on the wall and no skins on the floor. It felt more like a parlour, a room rarely used. Rena led me to her children, framed and displayed on the lid of the piano. She told me a little bit about the two older girls, who were no longer at home, and then she spoke about all the years that she'd waited for a son. After my four girls, she said, I was given a son, and we called him Danny-boy. He was exactly the son I wanted, with red hair and freckles. Rena was tall, with slender arms and legs, but she had a womanly shape, nicely heavy at the breasts and hips. She walked with a soft maternal roll, as the African women did. Her hair was curly and brown, and her eyes were dark in her olive skin. As she told me about her children, I felt that I could be her child too. Her heart was elastic enough to include me, and she knew how to be a mother. She was shaped like a mother and had a mother's smile. Just the thought that I might have found a real mother – not the river, not the bushveld, but a mother of the human kind – made me feel less unhinged, almost normal.

Coming from the kitchen, with its half-door open to the yard, I could hear African laughter. Venison was cooking slowly in the oven, and beneath the meat odours was a delicate, fragrant memory of the outdoors. Is there rosemary in the meat? I asked her. Ag, she said, delighted, you know how to cook already. I always put in rosemary and a small bay leaf. My mother has some rosemary, I explained, in our garden. Ah, she said, your mother taught you to cook? No, I said, looking off, my sister did. A radio was playing African music, which would not have been tolerated at home. I peeked into the kitchen; the women looked up and smiled and then turned back to their work. There were no houseboys at the farm, only Damara women working in the kitchen. They were conspicuous as peacocks in their Victorian-style cotton dresses, with tight bodices and wide, layered, red, blue and yellow floating skirts. They'd come from Namibia a century before, at a time when it had belonged to Germany, and went right on wearing the dresses of their oppressors. There they were, working in the bright kitchen, looking like throwbacks to another era. Their faces were serene and beautiful beneath intricately folded doeks that were studded with large, glittering brooches.

Come, Rena said, you'll get to know them and they'll find a name for you. We walked together down a long corridor with room after room leading off it – past the bedroom Rena shared with Dan le Cordeur, past a small bathroom, and then into a long dormitory with four low beds lined up. Between each bed was a chest of drawers with a crocheted doily in the middle of the pale wood. Sky and sunlight came through small, high windows, making blue squares in the white walls. The house was just a long string of rooms with a passageway connecting them, and it felt like a warehouse, which was what it had once been. The leg of the L had been added on – to name it after the inhabitants and to anoint it with luck.

From the first day it seemed to me that Rena was attending to my wounds. Her kindness, and even the softness of her voice, was hard to take at first and, as if to warn her, I'd blurt out that I was a bad child, or suggest weakly that I didn't deserve the little presents she showered on me: a little box made of seashells, a slim ivory bracelet, a little gold cow with a green eye. She turned to me with a puzzled look and said, but how can there be a child that's bad?

It was lunchtime, and she'd locked up the store for an hour and came back to see how I was getting on at the house. The two of us were in the kitchen and she was making me a sandwich on thick, white homemade bread spread thickly with butter and chutney. As she laid on slices of cold venison and little slivers of onion and cucumber, she was watching me. I stood a little awkwardly beside her. She always let the servants go home to the kraal for lunch, and without them the big kitchen seemed very quiet. The heavy old-fashioned stove belted out heat like a train. Only the two of us were at home. The three girls – Myfanwy, Angela and Vyvyan, who was my age, were off at the lands with Dan le Cordeur. I'd decided to stay behind. I wouldn't even go to the store with Rena when she'd asked me to. Sit, she said, you've been alone here all morning. Why didn't you go with the others? I need to be by myself, I said. She nodded, but said nothing. I'm not used to being with people, I said, before shoving my face deep into my sandwich. Ja, she said gently, but you'll get used to us, don't worry.

I couldn't get used to having so many people around. I didn't know quite how to relate to Vyvyan, who was quiet and sweet enough, but Myfanwy, her older sister, was unlike anyone I'd ever come across. She was dark and beautiful, and very intimidating. In the morning, she would sling a bra around her waist, slip her arms through the straps, and lean forward and tip her large bosoms down into the cups. Her ease with her body alarmed me. Her strong, clear voice, her laughter and utter confidence were shattering. I'd watch her with my mouth open. She could shoot a gun, drive a tractor, or any of the trucks, roll on the grass with the dogs, brand and castrate the cattle, and match her father at any damn thing. She was like a son to him without being in any way mannish.

Beside Myfanwy, the real son of the family fell into shadow. Danny-Boy – the long-awaited and much-loved son of his mother – was small for his age and very quiet. He seemed to inhabit a dream world and he stayed apart from us. In memory, he's hard to locate, as if he was on the rim of our lives, out of sight. He didn't even look like the rest of the family, and emotionally he didn't fit: internalized and guarded, off in his own head, he seemed afraid of his father.

I didn't much like Dan's way with him: you got the impression that he was trying to mash the poor kid into the ground. As Rena and I moved about in the kitchen, she didn't know where Danny-Boy was and that surprised me. Oh, it's okay, she said, he just goes off in the bush for a bit. He doesn't like to go to the lands, doesn't like the branding and castrating – that's what they're doing today. He goes off just before his dad turns up in the lorry to fetch the others. We're used to it now.

She shifted her gaze to my hacked-off hair. Do you like it this way, so short? she asked. Her daughters had hair all the way down to their waists. Vyvyan had long golden hair, which she yanked around to the front of herself every morning and plaited in two minutes flat. My mother wants my hair short, I said nervously, she doesn't let us grow our hair. Does she cut it herself, then? she asked, touching the ends, and then ran her hand down the back of my head. When you are here with us, she said slowly, must I let you keep your hair like this, because I myself can't cut hair very well. She was looking at me, and I jumped right in. Oh no, now I'm here I'll just have to let it grow. She nodded. Very well then, since that's what you've decided, we should brush it, every day and night, to make sure no tangles get into it. Look how fine and pretty your hair is, she smiled. It just hasn't had a chance to see itself that way. And, she said, noticing I'm sure that I stank like a polecat, I have some pine oil. Why don't you have a bath now that the house is all quiet, and put lots of oil in the water?

All I wanted to do was to be with Rena. When I was with her, she seemed to pull me in close to her side, keeping me safe. I'd walk with her every morning down the scruffy path set off by thorn scrub and stunted acacia trees and we'd open up the store together. It had a low stoep overlooking the main road where the Africans sat waiting, with their children and bundles, for her to come. Once the Africans were inside the store, they spent hours in there, out of the sun, surrounded by all the things they most longed to possess. They tested and compared the bolts of bright cotton, rubbing the fabric between their fingers like tobacco, and took down the heavy blankets and pots and pans and studied them carefully. They wanted to look, to touch and to admire. The floor space was almost entirely covered by sacks of mealie-meal, groundnuts, sugar and dried milk. Bicycle tyres and buckets and washboards hung from the ceiling. Children ran in and out of the doors, eyeing the jars of sweets in the glass displays. The days were long, and by the end of them Rena looked tired, with dark circles under her eyes. Why do you have to work here every day? I asked her. Because if I don't the store will be empty in no time: people, when they have nothing, steal. Ja, I would, too.

I sat by her side in the corner while she knitted. She had a ball of white wool, which she kept in a small muslin bag, and as her fingers raced over the clicking needles, she'd stop from time to time and sprinkle Johnson's Baby Powder over her fingers. This ritual helped to keep at bay the flies, the dust gathering on every surface, the noise, the smell and the dreariness of each day. I'd been sitting with her for a long time that day, on my little stool in the corner, and neither of us had said much – so heavy was the day, and so soporific the dry heat and mustiness of the store – when, looking at her soft skin and the lack of tension in her face, suddenly I blurted it out. I wish you were my mother, I said with a gasp. She didn't look up from her knitting, but she smiled a little and said in her slow, soft voice, How come, when you've got such a dainty little mother? The way she said it, and the smile she gave me, so without censure that it seemed forgiving, eased the enormity of my treachery.

One day a white man pulled up outside and came into the store. That will be Willie Swart, she said, without looking up. I looked at him with curiosity. White people only came into the store if they were strangers looking for directions. How goes it, missus? he said in Afrikaans to Rena. You knew he was Afrikaans by the shape of his head: it was flat on the top and his jaw was narrow but jutting. This shape, according to my father, was indicative of a very small brain. He had narrow, unhappy eyes surrounded by deep creases and his skin was very dark and dry. He began to complain – about the blacks, the British – about the lack of rain, about having nothing to feed his cattle with, and once he started he couldn't seem to stop.

Rena asked him about his wife. How's Bunny? she asked. I've been meaning to go and see her. I'll go today if she's there. She's there, he snapped, she's always there. Rena asked him if there was anything he wanted from the store and he rattled off his list, and then asked her to put it on the slate. She shook her head. There's a lot on the slate already, Willie. He got agitated. Look, man, I'll pay you at the end of the week, true as God. I'm getting rid of a few of my cows. Any day now I'll have the cash. Rena looked at him with a mixture of shame and pity, and then looked away. She said sharply to the black man listening, Go and put the baas's order in the back of his jeep. The black man smiled mockingly and went slowly to fill the order.

Later that day, when it was cooler, we went to see Willie Swart's wife. I wanted to go because I knew their son, Dawie Swart. He went to school with me at Miss Klopper's at Gabs, where he lived with her because things were such a shambles at home. I'd heard the story, but no details. He was the boy who gave me my first bouquet, but he never spoke, though I knew he could. Rena took the bakkie and we drove out into the bush a bit and down a potholed road that led to a rusty gate. When I opened it, we drove down a rutted track overgrown by weeds and blackjacks. At the end of the dirt road was a solitary farm, raising mealies and a small herd of cattle. The cattle were nearly all gone; only a few scrawny cows remained. On one side of the house we could see weeds taking over and strangling the mealies; they were stunted and small, and would come to nothing. A few chickens that had not yet been stolen squawked and ran all over the place. A dead creeper was dripping its brown rag across the windows of a dilapidated house with a gauzed stoep in front. A few savage dogs growled at us but ran when I threw a stone at them. Piano music was coming out of one of the open windows; it sounded plaintive and sad. She plays that piano all day long, Rena said. We'll go in in a bit, but I don't want you to be scared. This is Davie's mum, and she's not very well. I know, I said, they say she's a lunatic. Ja, well, people say things, Rena said, but how can we know the mind of another, or what suffering has done to it?

Rena called a few times, but no one came, so she took me by the hand and we just pushed open what was left of the screen door and followed the music. Mrs Swart, or Bunny – which I knew to be an English name – was sitting on a stool in front of a grand piano. The lid of the piano was propped open with a limb of a mopani tree. A woman was sitting there in a grimy, dark dress, bent forward over the keys, swaying a little, her head tilted to one side. We stood at the door and watched her for a bit, and I looked at the walls that seemed to be caving in, and the mounds of droppings all over the floor. The sand had drifted in and made soft piles in the corners; ragged tufts of thornscrub lay here and there like rough wreaths. Rena leaned close to me and whispered: she used to play at the church, and also at children's parties, but after it first happened, she couldn't any more, and then when it just carried on, she couldn't see people, and no one came near her after that. After what? I hissed. Rena seemed not to have heard. I think she plays to keep herself alive out here, as the bush creeps closer, and the mealies collapse in the dirt, and the thorn bushes grow higher on the road. Willie doesn't come here any more; nobody comes here any more. Rena was talking about the woman as if she couldn't hear, as if she wasn't there at all, and it bothered me.

The woman at the piano turned. Rena held my arm, almost as if she wanted to keep me a little back, behind her, as she herself moved closer and spoke reassuringly. It's all right, Bunny, we've just come to see you for a bit, not to worry. Bunny didn't seem to hear. Her hair must once have been gold like my mother's, but now it was streaked with white, and it was mangy and thin. Her English complexion had curdled and her pale blue eyes looked like the eyes I had seen once in the face of a very old black man, bleached and blind. Her eyes reflected defeat of the most lonely and terrible kind, but when she spoke she had an English voice, refined, the tone elevated and musical. How kind of you to come, she said. Won't you sit down? When we looked around us – there wasn't a thing to sit on – she got up and offered us her piano stool. I was out of there in a flash, my heart banging against my ribs, my head spinning. The emptiness of her gaze, that thousand-yard stare, was more than I could take.

When Rena came back out into the sunshine, I was inside the truck, looking out of the window at nothing. She sat for a moment before turning on the ignition. Did she spook you then? she asked me, rubbing my arm. I nodded. I'm sorry, she said, I didn't realize how bad she's got. Her voice was flat and final. I hesitated for a full minute and then I asked her. Is that what a lunatic who's English looks like? I stared hard at her as she thought for a while. What do you think it means to be a lunatic? Do you think they look a certain way? I couldn't answer; I didn't know; I was just terrified.

Driving out of the gate, leaving the mangled vines and the collapsing stoep behind us, we came upon the kraal where Willie Swart's labourers lived with their families. Dogs barked and chased our lorry, and some Africans lifted their faces and watched us pass with expressionless stares. A small band of piccanins began to run after the truck, shouting and waving. I noticed, with shock, that one of the kids was white, and then I saw another white one, a tiny girl this time, running in the dust with the black kids. Hey, I said to Rena, craning my head around to look back, there are white ones back there. No, she said, they're not white. I looked again. They weren't like the albinos who hid up in the koppies and got stoned if they came down to the village. I'd seen those. These were white kids. But, I protested, they're as white as me. No, she said, they're not white. They're nothing. I turned to her and stared. How can there be a child that's nothing? I asked her. She looked down and away, her face flushing.

She had to slow down because the road was full of deep holes. The running kids were closer to us now and one of them, a small boy of about eight, ran up very close to the lorry and then stopped; his face shook with a spasm of hatred, and he picked up a stone and hurled it savagely at the lorry. It clipped my side with a hollow explosion. Rena kept on driving, but her mouth and jaw stiffened. We said nothing. On we drove, past another kraal nestling into a peaceful evening ritual. Children were bringing in the cattle and goats, and fires burned as the sun dipped lower in the sky. Willie Swart is a drinker, Rena said, as if that explained everything. When I continued to look at her, she said, those kids you saw are his. He sleeps with kaffir women.

Eight

FOR SOME REASON, DAN LE CORDEUR TOOK A SHINE TO ME.
He got up Angela's nose in no time, but he had a kind of
energy that I liked – and besides he was nice to me. So
whenever I could drag myself away from Rena, he encouraged me to come out on the lands with him and see the
farm. He called me 'groen oogies'. One day, my girl, he
said, those green eyes of yours are going to drive young
men to despair – better watch out, hey? When I sat next to
him in the truck, he told me how he'd dragged the farm out
of the thin soil – ploughed and planted and bought cattle,
bred them and sold them, slowly building up a good herd.
This is the only land, he said, only this little strip of it, on
this side, that's worth a damn. Anywhere else nothing
grows. I made it here only by the skin of my teeth, I'm
telling you, and I had to do some things to get where I am
that I wouldn't want your dad and his crowd of rooineks to

know about. Ag no, then I'd be in big trouble. He squinted at me. Money had to change hands, he said cautiously, and other things took place. He didn't like my father, I could tell, and he didn't like his kind either. He wanted to be out there doing exactly what he wanted and he wasn't going to put up with any British restrictions and regulations.

I thought at first nothing would grow here, he said, and the cattle I could get my hands on were worthless. Those first years, I'm telling you, poverty's not the word for it; we were in the same boat as the kaffirs. The house had nothing in it, so we slept on the floor, ja, no word of a lie, we had nothing. I had one shirt to my name, and a wife who was always trying to get it off my back to give to someone else. I tell you, those were not days I'd have again. The kaffirs were cheeky and lazy; we were ploughing with some ancient thing pulled by oxen – ja, like back in the old days. He laughed. Nobody believes me now, how it was then. I didn't think we'd make it, true as God, and we wouldn't have, if not for my angel, we wouldn't have got through those days without Rena. She was working right alongside me, down in the dirt planting the first mealies, hoping to God the drought wouldn't keep up, and she was big then, ja, those babies kept coming, and she just kept on working right beside me, just like she does now, except now she's in the store. One time, when the doctor came to deliver her, we thought she'd die, ja, it was that close, and the doctor he turned to me and said, Dan, which one must I save, your wife or the child? I looked at him and said, Save them both, and hurry up about it. There she was, my angel, my darling, lying in terrible pain, her face all damp and blue and he's asking me a stupid bleddy question like that. Save them both, I told him. And he knew better than not to do so.

He sped along over the rutted roads, keeping up a steady stream of conversation, looking out across his lands as if he was still astonished that all this was really his. His window would be open, with his elbow stuck in it, an arm reaching up and tapping on the rooftop. His hair was golden and curly; he had fierce amber eyes and a wide, seductive smile that dimpled up his cheeks. He was a small man, tightly constructed and compact, but so strong and muscled that he seemed ample. Every so often he would brake in front of a gate and I would jump out, unhook the wire loop, push the gate open, and swing on it to the other side, then close it again and jump back in. Did you close it good? he would ask each time, at each gate. I'd nod. You'd better have, or there'll be hell to pay. As we drove along the undulating roads, sometimes we'd come across a few African kids with a goat or two and he'd stop and speak to them in Setswana, asking where they were going. He always knew which village they came from and he called them by their names. I know all my kaffirs, he said. We live close-close with them, like a family. They love me like a father, and I them as my children.

Once in a while, a kid would climb up on the back of the lorry; sometimes a woman with a load on her head would flag him down and get a ride. If he came across a stray animal, he'd check to see if his brand was on it, and if it was sick or small, he might heave it up on to the back of the lorry. Once he found a cow with a broken leg and he got out of the lorry and shot it dead. One time, when we were in a gully, looking for a goat that had given birth, a mamba crossed his path and he blew its brains out just like that.

The sjambok at my feet shifted in the dirt as the lorry lurched about. The stiff handle and the thin whip made of rhino hide had a knot at the end, which would take out a small piece of flesh, round and deep as a pea. The sjambok always began its journey with the whip wound tightly around the handle, but soon it broke free and lay sprawled at my feet, coiling and uncoiling with the lorry's agitation. I kept my feet away from it, and he noticed this, observant as he was, and laughed. You're scared of that thing, hey? I'll teach you how to use it and then you won't be scared any more. I must teach you also how to shoot and then when we go out at night on the lands you can have your own kill. Ja, you'll like that? Your very own kill.

On one of these trips out to the lands Dan explained to me how it was, how he saw it. You see, my girl, with a country like this, with a people like this, someone has to be the boss. Ja. It's like with the kaffir dogs that come to us – one day he's out there in the bush, and the next he's on the edge of my yard, looking in, starving, his bones stuck to his backbone. He's not seen water or food for days and he comes in from the bush only because he must, or he'll die. So what must I do with this wild dog? He's not yet out of his own evolution, and he's got a long way to go. So there he is, in my yard, looking at me with wild eyes, crazy with hunger, his haunches dropped and his head down. I see him and I hate him for what he is. I hate the way he looks. He hates me, too. If he could, he'd kill me, but he knows I'm the superior animal. And if he doesn't, then I must show him.

So what must I do? He's just a piece of the wild trying to come in. What must I do? He turned and looked at me, and when I didn't answer, he answered for me. I must tame him, that's what I must do, and I can't tame him unless I fight him, break him, make him see who's the master. Ja. I have to fight him with my bare hands and make him submit and then that way there's peace between us. And I do this, my girl, not out of the cruelty of my heart, but only because if he comes close to my door, he's a danger until he's broken. He'll kill my chickens and bite the piccanins, he'll fight with my dogs and tear up the pens to get at the pigs. No, if he enters my domain, then I must make him submit to it, and to do that I must fight him with my bare hands. I looked at him. How can you fight him with your bare hands without him biting you? Ag, man, he said, first I must stop up his mouth, and also I must hobble his legs, or take the sjambok to him, but most of all I must fill him with the fear of God, so that something in him is already broken before even I touch him. But then, when he's broken, I asked him, what then? Ag, he smiled widely, then I have an animal I can keep in my yard.

Sometimes, he said softly, ja, sometimes he'll pretend that he loves me, but true as God, he loves me not. When he licks my hand it's to get the salt, only that. There is no love between us, only obedience. And then one day the moment comes when the gate is off the latch, and his belly is propvol, and he goes back to where he came from. He goes deep-deep into the veld to where he's really free, just like the old Boers did when they fled from the Englishers. He, too, must go back because there is where he belongs and there is where he must always return.

We'd got to the lands. Rows and rows of mealie plants shuddered like stacked spears in the clear air. It was stinking hot, heading for noon. Black men sat under a few sparse trees, squatting on their knees, their heads hanging. We drove into their midst with a rush of dust. The tyres snarked in the sand, and their faces lifted for a moment. Dan was out like a whip, looking at the men squatting in the sand. Some got to their feet and brushed themselves off; others bent to pick up their hoes. Dan strutted in that way he had, like a boxer, his arms parrying the air. Where's my boss-boy? he yelled. Where the hell is he hiding? He spun on those still sitting. And why are you kaffirs sitting in the shade still? Do you think that maybe I'm bringing lunch and beer? He was good-humoured, trying to jolly them along. Always he kept moving. Or did you forget that the lorries are coming at one o'clock? Or maybe you kaffirs thought it was Sunday, hey? They were flat and listless, exhausted – in a trance that no word of his could break.

The boss-boy came walking over from the edge of the field, where the green met the dun earth. He walked slowly. He was tall, loose-limbed, naked to the waist, his skin streaked with sweat and his face grey from the heat. On his head, shielding it from the sun, was what had once been a white handkerchief. Now, grimy and soft with grease, it was pulled tightly over the crown of his head and knotted at the corners. He stood in front of Dan. Baas? he said simply. Dan turned his full attention on him. Johannes, what's going on here, man? He pointed in the direction of the green lake quivering in the heat. This field's not cleared, and I want you kaffirs to help out with the branding later. The man said, we will finish it, baas. His hands were loosely clasped in front of him. How then can you finish it if you're sitting on your backsides? Can you tell me that, man? We will finish, baas, the man repeated, but he was surly, his eyes hooded, his face slightly averted, though not enough to cause offence. Dan swatted a fly on the back of his neck. A triangle of sweat had formed between his shoulders and spread, darkening the cloth. He was bare-headed, and the short curls began to dampen at the back of his neck. He was shorter than the other man, but he began to move with a kind of swagger, looking from the field to Johannes. Suddenly he strode over to the field, and entered it, so that he was enclosed in green. He crouched down and began to yank at something, his broad back shaking the mealie plants. He stood, and with a handful of tangled dry weed and blackjack in his hand, he came back and shoved it in the other man's face. He butted himself closer. Do you want that I should water these, too? Hey? That I should use my good water pumped up from my boreholes to let the whole bleddy veld and every useless weed on it drink? The black man was silent. Johannes repeated, we will finish, baas.

Dan exploded with irritation. Now – now you're promising me to work, when the day's half gone and the sun's high. He pointed to the others. You're telling me that you can get them to work? Do you think I'm a domkop? They've been drinking kaffir beer all night; they won't wake up till tomorrow. Already it's too late for this field. And on Friday, when it's time for wages, you'll be ag, please, baasie, with your hand out, isn't it? He stood very close to the black man, who seemed still to be sleeping, and he shoved him, making contact with the gleaming, wet shoulder, where he left a dry, dull handprint. A small tremor ran over Johannes's chest. Dan took a step back, but at the same time took up a pose, his fists raised a little, his feet shuffling in the dirt, knees bent – a pugilist, poised and waiting. The fire went out in the black man, his body sagged, and his eyes dropped to the ground.

Who's the boss here? Do you want my job? Hey? Is that it? Come on, then, take it from me. Let's see you act like a man. Dan moved back, but took up his fighting position again. Come on, let's fight it out, man to man, and get it over with. Dan danced a little in the dirt. The other stood looking out across lands not his, cattle not his, mealies growing in the sun that would not reach his belly, but instead would be sold across the border. He shrugged, barely. The men under the trees all stood now, close together, watching. There was apprehension in the air and a kind of excitement – the kind that ripples down your spine when you're watching a lion about to spring at an impala's throat. The flies buzzed, the minutes drained away as the two men stood there under the omnipotent sun. Then Dan threw a punch, light, almost sweet, as if he was just trying it out, just playing, and it landed on the other's chest. Come on, then, fight like a man, he crooned, but not the way you kaffirs like to fight – to kill a man, to smash his brains in. Fight like a white man and I won't hold it against you. Johannes lifted his head. His eyes were clear and focused. Baas, I only know one way to fight, and that's to kill a man and smash his brains in.

When next I dared to look, the two of them were in a locked embrace, the tall black man towering over the white one, a knotted dark arm held like a rod against the back of a thick, white neck. Dan ducked quickly and pulled back enough to catch Johannes on the side of his face, and then he began to beat the living daylights out of his stomach and chest. Johannes didn't fight back. It was as if he was simply trying to hold Dan off, almost without touching him, as if the intimacy of their closeness was less tolerable than the blows. Again and again Dan hit him, harder and more deeply. I watched him, fascinated, and I couldn't believe that the black man wasn't fighting back. I was furious with him, bitter against him because I knew that he could. As Dan felt the resistance hollow out, he seemed to fight in a new way and it was then that I realized that he was fighting the way a kaffir fights, to kill a man and smash his brains in.

I couldn't look after that, and when I peered out from between my hands again, Johannes was sprawled in the dirt, covered in blood. When I looked at the scarlet against the black, it had a great beauty and I couldn't take my eyes off it. For a moment it seemed as though Johannes was going to get up. His body turned and he pushed himself up with one arm, wiping the blood from his eyes. On his skin, the blood had mingled so evenly with the black wetness of his flesh that they seemed one colour. I saw his face and he had that look, that wanting to kill, it was there, it was there, and my heart began to beat wildly, to urge him on, to whisper, do it, do it now. But suddenly Dan moved. He let down his arm and raised Johannes from the dirt. The two stood a moment, facing one another, and then the black man stooped to pick up his handkerchief and replace it on his head. With blood running from a gash above his eye, his face seemed liquid, and he looked down at the dirt, where small splashes of scarlet fell at his feet.

Dan strolled back to the lorry, and to me. He started the engine, and then leaned out the window and called out: You make sure then that this field is cleared before the lorry comes, you hear me now? I hear you, baas, Johannes said. The men under the trees shuffled and stirred, and then moved slowly towards the field, their backs bent against the heat. In the front seat, I didn't look at Dan, or he at me. He was a mess. He must have been down in the dirt too, because his clothes were filthy and there was blood on his sleeve, though I didn't know whose blood it was since there's no difference. I was so furious that I wanted to hit him. What's eating you then? he asked, his voice low. There was something about him that looked different to me. He seemed small, and I didn't like that. He rallied quickly, pulling himself back into a good humour, shoving a hand through his hair, and he gave a quick laugh, triumphant and full. That field will be cleared by the time the lorries get there, no worry. I gave him a hiding he won't forget. He took out a neatly ironed handkerchief and wiped his face. He let you win, I said, looking out of the window. Dan was silent a long while and then he said, Don't tell me, my girl, that you're going to end up one of those kaffirboeties? He gave me a warning look. If you start to love the kaffir, go out there with him, but you better remember there's no way back. I shook my head: I was no different from anyone else, no different from him, but that didn't stop me hating him.

I wanted to hate him so badly, but I couldn't, and pretty soon he'd wangled his way back into my affection through sheer ebullience. He was so alive, so at one with where he was that he was part of it, so how could I hate him without hating all of it? Let's go to the dam, he said, and take a dip. I can't go home to my angel looking like this. Immediately I tensed up; immediately he'd become creepy. I knew what this taking a dip business was all about. One day we'd stopped at one of the reservoirs on the way home. Dan liked to swim naked, and he liked to swim naked with his daughters. He'd done it since they were little, and maybe when they were little it was okay. That day, as they stripped off and hung their clothes up in the trees, I walked away by myself. I stayed down on the ground as they climbed up the ladder into the circular cement tank, which rose about ten feet from the ground. I could hear the three of them – Myfanwy, Vyvyan and him – laughing and splashing as they swam and cooled off. Angela wouldn't go in either. She walked off and sat under a tree. We two ignored each other. They called to us to come and join them, but we didn't budge. Now, when he suggested it again, I got into a panic. I don't have my swimming costume, I said. He snorted like a horse. Hell, what's the matter with you, hey? What's the problem with you and your sister that you can't go starkers like the rest of us? Come on, he whacked my arm lightly. Let's just go in for a bit so I can get some of this kaffir blood off me. He laughed. You can keep your broeks on if you want. I squeezed myself up in the corner, near the door, and reached for the handle. You Englishers, he laughed, you're surely an odd bunch. He pulled over and parked under a willow close to the dam, and he was out and, no doubt, starkers in no time. He dived straight in and his arms cut through the brown water as he made his way to the island in the middle. The black boys kept skimming stones over the water and the wild duck kept on flying through the cloudless sky. Only I, with my back turned, sat miserably in the dirt, chopping at the hard earth with a stone, itchy with heat and inflamed by the sun – furious with him and the whole damned stinking world.

Nine

EVERY EVENING ON THE FARM A LONG TRESTLE TABLE WAS
laid out on the grass beyond the veranda, and we all
gathered together to eat. We said grace – or rather Dan did
– and then he stood before a huge piece of meat, and
carved. Slabs of venison or beef were served up with rice
and roast potatoes – white and sweet – beans and
pumpkins, squash and corn, thick slices of white bread and
brown gravy. Farm or family matters would be discussed as
the stars came out one by one. And as twilight came and the
bugs clustered around the lightbulbs on the stoep and it got
a bit colder, so sometimes you had to go in to get a jersey or
a cardigan, or even to put on socks. At these times, Danny-
boy was with us. He was quiet, and there was often a
tension between him and his father. Sometimes Dan would
start in on him. Why didn't you come to the lands today?
He'd wave his knife. I like you to see how we spay. We did

five hundred head. Danny just kept on eating, slowly and without enthusiasm. Listen, boy, I'm speaking to you. Yes, Pa, I heard. Well, then, you know I don't push you on the branding and the castrating, not now, because you're still small, but later these things will be part of your life. Who's going to run this farm when I'm gone? Tell me that?

The boy seemed so placid, so dreamy, and yet he was angry. I could tell it in the way he held his hands together on his lap and clenched his knees. He wanted to be let alone; just being near his father unmanned him. He wasn't interested in chasing the kaffir dogs, learning to shoot, riding the horses, or branding and castrating the cattle. If Dan kept on at Danny-boy too long, Rena, at the other end of the table, would frown, and he'd stop, but not until he'd made his remarks about sissies and nancy-boys. Whenever he did this, Vyvyan would try somehow to steer the conversation another way, but he'd get back to it. Look at your sisters, he'd say to Danny, be more like them. Never would I have thought I'd say that to a son of mine. But after the lemon meringue pie, or the milk tart, or the koeksisters, Dan would settle himself on the long, green, upholstered swing and ask Danny-boy to fetch his ukulele. Then, as the Damara women cleared the table, he would begin to strum, and the tension would be long gone. Dan's voice would boom out 'My Old Man Says Follow the Band', and 'Sally', and 'Sarie Marais', and the sound of the swing's creaking and the clatter of the ukulele filled the silent night, drowning the song of the cicadas and the baying of the hyenas out beyond the kraal. He and Rena sat there side by side, his thigh pressed close to hers, and looking at them, he so golden, she so dark and still, it was as if they'd divided their universe in half, so that she, his angel, his darling, in her goodness and simplicity, could afford him the indulgence to do whatever he wished.

On other nights, the eating was over and done with in no time, and we went shooting on the lands. We'd wrap up well and climb up on the back of the blue lorry, with guns and rugs and a flask of brandy. Rena didn't come with us; she'd wait up till everyone came home and then make hot coffee and rusks for us. The lorry rumbled off to the lands – Myfanwy up in the front with her father, the rest of us on the back, hanging on to the grille for dear life, banging into one another as the lorry rolled on the rutted road. Dan drove like a madman, and we four, Angela, me, Vyvyan and Danny-boy, looked out over the cab of the lorry at the white moonlit road and took turns jumping off to open and close the gates. And he said the same things to them as he said to me. Did you close it good? You'd better have, or there'll be hell to pay. When we got to the lands, the lorry slowed down, and Danny-boy pulled out a large torch, and trained it on the far fields, so that we could look for the eyes of the buck. You didn't have to wait long. Impala eyes were quite different from the crazed and crafty red eyes of the night crocs at Maun; those eyes were monstrous, like burning coals in a face made of iron. The buck's eyes were small and they glowed like rubies or single pomegranate seeds. The pinpricks of light were all you could see of their triangular faces and soft ears as the beam travelled through the darkness, seeking out death.

Dan would slow down from time to time and make cracks about being in lion country, or he'd stop just to tell us that someone had seen an elephant or cheetah up a bit, where the ravine was. That shut us up. We looked up at the sky, dark and moonless. Hold the light up, for God's sake, Dan would call out, they don't keep their eyes in their knees. Danny-boy raised the beam, or, more likely, Vyv took it from him. But just when we were made dreamy by the darkness and the stars, we would see, way out in the bush, two silver sparks caught and held in the beam of the light. One of us banged on the roof of the cab, and the engine cut out quietly. The steady light had hypnotized the springbok, stunning it into stillness, and we could see the outline of its shape, and even the soft white of its belly, waiting, as if it knew. Myfanwy dipped her shoulder, raised her shotgun, aimed, and fired. The night cracked open, the sparks went out, and then you heard the thud. I got him, Myfanwy said, with casual approval. Eland, don't you think, Dad? Ja. Bull, he said. Myfanwy got out and strode off into the bush, her hips swaying, the light of the torch cutting a golden swathe through the dark field. Angela followed and soon caught up with her. Go with them, Dan said to Danny-boy, help bring it back. Vyvyan jumped down. I'll go, she said. No, Dan insisted, Danny must go. The boy trailed off across the field, but didn't try to catch up with the other two. I swear to God, Dan said, in exasperation, that boy will end up a vegetarian the way he's carrying on.

While they were dragging the buck back, Dan gave me lessons in how to shoot a gun. He trained the light on the opposite field and we waited. It was very dry and the game had come close in, so pretty soon I could see a small buck, outlined by the light, close to us. Dan gave me a shotgun. Keep your eyes on the place. Don't move, he ordered. He pulled me close against him and then moved round so he was a bit behind me, holding my arm, settling the gun on my shoulder, steadying me. Okay now, look through the scope and hold it up a bit, like I showed you. Close one eye – no, the other one, domkop. Hold still, stop moving away from me, I'm not going to bite you. Jesus, what a jumpy little thing. Hold still, or you'll miss. Okay, that's good. Now. Fire. FIRE, for God's sake. Do you want I should ask him to come a bit closer for you? I missed. He laughed. Jesus! Did I tell you to close both eyes? If I'd wanted a blind person to shoot with me tonight I'd have brought oubaas along.

I couldn't shoot with him standing right up against me like that, but I began to practise by myself, or sometimes with Vyvyan, who was a pretty good shot, on the target on the lawn. I liked shooting, I liked the weight of the gun, and after a while it stopped kicking me in the shoulder. Looking at the round target, I'd imagine a face where the rings were, and that way I got to be rather accurate. Soon I began to feel a sense of exhilaration about firing the gun; it gave me the sense of belonging to a long line of hunters, warriors – a brave order of men. I thought that if I could get to be a really good shot, then maybe I could shoot my father in the head and call it an accident, the way white people did in the B.P. At first it was a joke, or I told myself it was a joke, but then slowly, as I practised more and got pretty good, it was less of a joke.

We were in the middle of a drought. The farm was dusty and woebegone – not a drop of rain for over a year. The Africans kept watching the sky and sometimes we'd all get excited as the air became heavy with electricity and the wind picked up. Clouds piled up, and then slipped away, and tiny, jagged flickers of lightning cut into a vibrating sky, or a volley of thunder rolled. The chickens got pulled into it too, and climbed up on their roosts in the middle of the day. Everything went quiet. In the kraal, the women kept up the rain dances and the witch doctor worked over-time, chanting and praying. The sand blew, and lonely thorn bushes whirled and then came to rest under the trees. But no rain fell. The signs went away and life dragged on. The jigsaw cracks in the earth deepened until it was like walking on stone. The water in the dams and reservoirs was getting dangerously low, the fodder in the silos was half gone. The thorn trees were fragile, gaunt as burnt sticks. Dan was edgy as a hornet.

I had trouble of my own. My time was nearly up: my mother and father were coming back, and for all the time they'd been away, I'd been living as if they wouldn't return. I'd forgotten them. I'd put that other life out of mind: it was gone as if it had never been. And then, shockingly it seemed, Rena had shown me a letter from my mother. They'll soon be home, she said, just three or four days. They were taking the Blue Train from Cape Town to Johannesburg and then would drive to Gabs and come and take us home. Would you like to read the letter? Rena asked me. Shame, your mother must miss you. Seeing my mother's writing on the envelope brought me right up against a reality I'd put aside. I wouldn't read the letter. It was hard at first to conjure up my mother's face, and when I thought of my father I only saw the target on the lawn, with the punctured green and yellow rings and the bull's-eye in the centre. In that short time – it was only a measly two months – another life had blossomed – another world that, like Maun, would soon be gone.

I thought I could just forget my other life until I collided with it. But this time, I couldn't quite vanish it. I kept getting flashes of my mother's averted, tense face, or my father's hands, the hair on his arms, the top of his head. When I saw these images, my stomach toppled, my head reeled and I thought I'd faint, or I began to think that I was having dizzy spells or neuralgia. I had to get away and be by myself: I had to seal off the leak that had begun in my mind. I headed for the bush, shoeless and hatless, walking out beyond the sheds and storehouses, beyond the deserted dam, beyond the fences and out, out, out to where there was nothing. The trees in the distance wobbled, illusive water rippled up ahead of me, endlessly vanishing, endlessly returning, but in the end, not there at all. On and on I walked, not feeling the scald of the sun, nor the sharp spines of small dead creatures half-buried in the sand. Heat flared up from the ground and boomed down from the heavens, and I walked till I couldn't walk any more. I crouched under a tree and let my head fall between my knees the way the Africans did. I felt dizzy and weak, and I thought I could just lie there and dry out, turn into dust and be blown away.

But then, as the glare bore down and the sun reached its zenith in the sky, I looked up and it seemed to me as if the sky did part, and the rain did come, for suddenly, out of nowhere, suddenly I knew I could go home. Something had changed and I was no longer who I'd been before. I was strong now, and free. I could shoot straight. I could take care of myself with the sjambok. If my father came near me, perhaps I could even kill him. For the first time, the thought of killing him filled me with pity – that I had such a father, that I was such a daughter. But I knew now that I could be another kind of daughter, the one I'd been to Rena on the farm, staying close to her in the dusty store, handing her things she needed, running back to the house to fetch her more wool, or a flask of tea. And I remembered how her face was never once turned to the wall, and her eyes, looking at me, never once had the thousand-yard stare of a woman pretending to be asleep.

*

When I felt this tenderness inside me, it made me powerful. And it was as if there was good, strong African blood in me now, as if out there in the bush I was turning into a primitive and that was making me ferocious and alive and real. Black warriors had been here, in this very place, millions of them, running lightly under the same sky, lifting their naked feet, balancing their plumed spears, travelling silently over the denuded sand with its crust of jewels. I saw them again as they came running by, black as blood, frightful as snakes. I wanted to be one of them – to be a girl warrior with shiny sleek skin and a spear in each hand. I wanted to run on the air like a Bushman, without stopping for miles, way up ahead, outdistancing the world.

Ripping off my clothes, I threw them away, even my white broeks, and there I was, naked – starkers – in a world of my own making. I began to turn, slowly, majestically, letting my body scald, willing it to catch fire. I was walking on diamonds, letting their sharp beauty pierce and redeem me of evil once and for all. The vast emptiness of the desert so intoxicated me that I began to dance and spin, stamping my feet, arching my arms to the heavens. I was on fire. I was home. Nothing and no one could harm me again.

When I got back to the farm, Rena took one look at me and rushed me to the bath, rested me against the cool enamel, and let the taps run hard with cold water. She put in ice and she threw in a bottle of aspirins and stirred them around. She was frantic and loving as she put me to bed with a fan blowing on my naked body. She smoothed on calamine and I tried not to scream. When she poured it on and smoothed it over my scarlet skin, it was beautiful at first, pink and cool as ice-cream, but in just a minute, barely a minute, the lotion made no difference – I'd caught fire and now my flesh was cooked. The pain was so deep that I fainted. I drifted in and out of fever and sleep. Apparitions visited me. I woke up and screamed. She asked me no questions, and in any case, my lips were so swollen and cracked that I couldn't even whisper. She kept on bathing my head until my fever went down, and once I heard her whisper to Vyv, she's delirious. Is she going to be all right? She sat up with me all night, but I don't remember much about it except a sense of a sheltering presence by my side, or a soft hand on my brow, and someone to keep the ghosts out of my bed.

In the day, if someone came in, bringing light through the doorway, she'd say, quick, close that curtain, hurry, or she'll go blind. I lay there in darkness for two days, and whenever I looked up from the pillows, she was sitting beside me, knitting, or she'd be lifting muslin out of a white bowl, wringing it out, and laying it on my forehead. The witch doctor had given her a potion made from herbs and disgusting things, and she made me swallow it. If I cried a little, she'd say, tears will heal your face. Don't you worry, don't you worry. I won't leave you. Leaning closer to me, she'd whisper in her soft, clear voice, you're getting better, just sleep. I'll stay with you till morning. Not once did she say, how could you do this now? And with your mother coming? Not once.

When I was recovered a bit, Angela came to see me. She took one look at my skin, which was beginning to come off in chunks, and winced. She was standing at the end of my bed. I wasn't in the dormitory, but in a small room close to the storerooms and sheds. I was to return to this room one more time, just before we were about to leave Africa, but now, as she stood there, with her eyes anxious and a little forlorn, she asked me wearily, why do you have to do this? Don't think that they're going to let you stay here just because you're sick. When I said nothing, she said bitterly, well, you'd better get well quickly. Mummy's not going to want to take care of you the minute she gets back from England. They're going to be here in a day or two and she's definitely going to be in a bad mood if she sees you looking like this.

It was all moving too fast. I wanted to hold back the days. I tried to fall back into that dream state and forget the future the way I had the past. But I couldn't. It seemed that my time in the bush had changed all that. I'd been burned, and I couldn't seem to return to the dreaming. Soon they would come and take us away and everything would be the same again. Angela and I were scrapping already. She was back in her reluctant role, worried and anxious, trying to smooth things out before we even got home. On the farm, I'd almost forgotten Angela along with my parents. Now she was stuck with me again. Back on duty. She'd taken over from Rena the minute she'd heard that our parents were on their way.

Ten

AS IT WAS, MY MOTHER CAME BACK ECSTATIC. SHE HAD A
bobbed hairdo and wore pink lipstick, not the usual dark
red, and her summer dresses – bought, not made – were
silky and sheer, or made of crisp linen. Wearing a dress like
this, dear, she'd say, one simply cannot sit down. She had
frocks with straight lines and elegant buttons and ones with
dropped waists. The skirts were shorter. More flattering
when one has the legs, she said, turning to look sideways in
the mirror. She had a cream suit with a cropped jacket and
round gold buttons, to meet visiting dignitaries, should
they come. She had three new pairs of high heels, and she
liked to wear them in the afternoon, when someone came
to tea. There she sat, in her chintz chair, folding and
unfolding her legs, making conversation as she sipped her
tea. She was transformed. Her afternoon bed was empty
now, the mosquito net rolled up into a loose knot like a

chignon, the fan stationary and silent. And if she even noticed my ruined face, she didn't say.

I heard her humming in the garden, and saw her smiling at my father, chatting to him in the drawing-room, as she straightened a picture or, checking for dust, ran her finger lightly over the surface of a table. She was busy, busy, busy – spending hours with her head in her cupboard, flinging out clothes and shoes, giving them away to the servants, with a stern admonition. Now, please take care of this, Elizabeth, it came from Harrods and it should last you a lifetime if you don't ruin it the way you tend to ruin most good things. She dived back into her cupboard and drew forth some shaggy dead animal. Oh, I can't imagine I would ever wear this again, she sighed, holding up a fox fur with the head left on. It was so elegant once, but now, well, it's just not the thing. Put it back in the mothballs, there's a dear.

I'd be lolling with my legs slung sideways over a chair. Please don't sit that way, she'd say, you'll break the arm. I really don't know what they were feeding you on that farm, but it's certainly gone to your hips. I sat up in the chair and bombarded her with questions: What's going on? Are we moving again? I tried to ask her questions that she was too preoccupied to answer, like, why do you keep chucking things out all the time? What's going on? Are we going to be moving again? I couldn't get an answer from her because I barely grazed her consciousness. Then she'd suddenly notice me, take in my presence, and pounce. Where did you get that chocolate? You know you're not supposed to have sweets until after lunch. No, don't put it there, for God's sake, you'll get it all over the chair. And look at your hair. My God, I hadn't noticed how long it is. Go and get me the scissors right away. I won't have you looking like that another minute. And why's your skin all peculiar like that? Oh, I suppose that must be the remains of the sunstroke. What a silly thing to do. What could you have been thinking of? Did I tell you about the fancy-dress ball on the boat, dear, it was so lovely; we stayed up till two in the morning and the band just played on and on.

There'd been talk. Rumours. Speculation. All sorts of possibilities running up and down. Gabs was buzzing with it. Was it true that our days in the protectorate might be coming to an end? That we might even go back Home to England? No one wanted to say much, not wanting to jinx it, but there had been hush-hush talks in Whitehall, with tongues wagging in high places. It was being suggested that we pull out before we got pushed. My mother was beside herself: was it possible that her diabolical time in Hell would soon be over? Africa was on the move and it meant that we could go, indeed, would have to go, our duty done. She was going to a place she barely knew, and she could hardly wait. She was exhilarated and full of energy and that was all that mattered: Home at last. Dear God, may it be over at last. May it be soon.

My father didn't share her enthusiasm. What the hell was he going to do with himself in England? He'd been through that before. And what did the stupid wogs think they were going to do without us? The place would be a shambles in a week, nothing would work in a month, and before you knew it the whole place would have gone back to the bush. On the other side of the tracks, a different story was running around. Independence was looming. Freedom was on the way. Messages came down through the jungles and plains, crossed the rivers and reached the villages; beaten out on drums, one drum taking over from the next, the message was passed on. The whites were going down. Time was up. It was 1958, barely two years before the Congo blew.

In those last months in Gabs, as he saw the future slipping out of his control, my father's anger was right up there on the surface, ready to explode at the least provocation. It's possible that he didn't know what was going to happen to him after the Gabs posting, and by then he must have been uncertain of what would come out of this, his second colonial career. Would he be yanked out of Africa and sent home to nothing – would it be that all over again? He'd once had hopes of being promoted to Resident Commissioner. There was only one of these, unlike district commissioners, who were ten a penny. And he'd cherished a dream that when his long service to the British government was over, there might even be a knighthood. Neither was to come to pass. He had problems with his superiors. He was too much of a loaded gun for people to want to have around.

He was going through a tough time, and he was taking it

out on me, the way he'd always done. After that brief time of clarity, at the farm, of being right there, alive and present, I split again: one part of me closed off at night, while the other rose in the morning to spend my days in a zombie state. Once I was in my father's house again, the edges of memory blurred and faded, and I moved back into shadow. I returned to the life I'd banished while I was on the farm. I went to school at Miss Klopper's, where I saw Dawie Swart again. But now I ignored him, now I knew too much about him and about his mother and father, and about those white kids who weren't white, but who were his brother and sister all the same. I didn't want anything to do with him. I didn't want him to know that I knew and had seen. I cut off from everyone. I ignored Susan completely, never touched her. Angela was away at boarding school, so I put her out of mind. I was ugly and bitter again, my hair hacked, my face hooded. I wasn't buying my mother's change of heart, not this time. I turned away from her, clutching my disappointment, furious and deadly as a snake.

But because I could smell my father's weakness, and because my own hatred was right back up on the surface, I knew it was my moment to strike. My father had had a few successes in Gabs; he'd organized the building of a club there and also written a report about the cattle and meat industry in the colony. He was very proud of this report, and so one day I remarked, with the casual violence learned at his knee, that his report was a failure. He began to haemorrhage on the spot. I'd struck deep into that hole inside him that made him the way he was. He couldn't recover. He refused to believe that I could make up something like that. I must have heard it from someone, and so this was how people really felt about the report; his work was not respected and nor was he. He couldn't assuage his sense of persecution and he couldn't let it be. On and on he raged, convinced that people were mocking him behind his back. It was like the times in England when he would mow the lawn to within an inch of its life, or chop down a tree as though it had personally offended him.

The report incident was such an astounding coup for me that I actually felt badly for him. I wanted to say I'd lied, but of course I couldn't. It was the first time I understood that I was threatening to him and that unless he could beat us all into submission, he was like a limp cobra nailed to a tree. Things went from bad to worse in Gabs. Something was eating him and the tension in the house was unbearable. I was becoming desperate: the splitting off had become so seamless that I found myself planning a murder – having feelings primitive and violent enough to fully imagine the deed – without fully understanding why. I was bewildered by the extent of my rage towards him. It seemed excessive even to me. I was terrified of him, but I didn't quite understand why I hated him so much. I was his daughter, his own flesh and blood, but he gave me the creeps whenever I was near him. I couldn't look at him. His hands repulsed me. The dark hair on his arms turned my stomach. His face, his voice and the way he ate made me want to stick a knife in him. But he was my father. I was supposed to love him, wasn't I? I couldn't think of love in connection with him, but I loved him. Didn't I? Did I? My confusion about him had been there for as long as I could remember and as I grew older it only got worse.

I didn't understand how things had got so bad unless I'd got so bad. That at least made sense. Sometimes I tried to help or please him in little ways, but the problem was too big. And because on the outside, to other people, of course he looked fine, so there was only one answer: I was the problem. It was obvious. My mother had washed her hands of me and of the volatile anger that passed between my father and me. She was concentrating on Susan. Susan was a good child, mild and golden-haired, and my mother could manage her. I could get into my mother's good books on those occasions when I was nice to Susan, or took care of her when she didn't want to be left with the servants, but I didn't want to do that because I was scared of what I might do to Susan if I was alone with her.

My mother made it clear to me that everything was my fault. She'd been telling me this for years: Why do you have to be so sullen, so unappealing? What's the matter with you? Why can't you be like other girls? She would lecture me as she sat in her full-length nylon slip in front of her dressing table, squinting into the mirror as she plucked at a stray eyebrow, or dabbed on some cream to lessen the dark circles under her eyes. English girls do not behave the way you do, she'd begin, they don't sulk and carry on all the time the way you do, or creep off into the bush and come back looking like a wild animal. No one will put up with you in England. Just look at you. You're a sight. You never wear shoes, your feet are like the natives', your hair's a rat's nest, you don't even wash yourself, you smell bad, you make people want to get away from you. What will people think when we get home?

Then she'd look in the mirror and stare miserably at her unpainted lips, and she'd flip back to her other self in a second. Oh GOD, she'd wail, I HATE this stinking bloody country, the heat, the dust, the filth everywhere you look. I can't stand it another minute. India was not like this. Simla was beautiful, the hills, the quiet nights. And Kashmir was lovely too – you could ski there or go out on the lake. India was not like this. India could be elegant and the people were intelligent, even after the massacres, killing each other that way, all that bloodshed and rioting, of course that was awful and we had to get out, but still, India was not like this.

She would peer at herself in the mirror, moving her face closer to the glass. She'd get into a panic: Look at my skin, my hair, what's happened to me? How can I go back looking like this? What will people think of me in England after all I've been through? I'd reassure her, calm her down, telling her that she was beautiful and no one would say anything bad, not a word. You know you look young, I'd say, people always tell you that you could be Dad's daughter because you look so young. I'd go to the kitchen and whip her up a face mask made from the whites of egg, and encourage her to take a nap. I'd help her tuck her curls in her hairnet, and hold the bowl as she smoothed on the mask and lay on the bed with her eyes closed. I'd fluff up the soft white mosquito net, and arrange it around her bed, and I'd promise to take Susan out of the house and into the garden to play so she could have a sleep. We will go back? she'd beg of me, we will get out of here, won't we? Yes, I nodded, we'll be packing in no time, not to worry, in no time we'll be gone.

The idea of leaving was a nightmare: getting out, going home, it was unthinkable. She was right about me, of course. She had me down pat. I can read you like a book, she always said. I couldn't go to England or anywhere else. Of course not. Nowhere else would accept me. Nowhere else would give me a second glance. I was as she'd described me. I couldn't survive anywhere else. Perhaps my father had similar thoughts, and he didn't want to face England any more than I did. We might have been some consolation to one another, but no such luck. Part of the time he treated me with utter indifference – I was the dust beneath his feet as he trampled on through, using the back of my neck as a resting place for his boot. India and Africa had shown him their indifference. My mother had learned how to return his indifference with her own brand, but all I had was my unvoiced rage, and a mounting urge to strike back, once and for all. The violence passing silently between the two of us became the psychic air that we breathed.

My mother didn't come to my defence when my father

became violent; she pretended it wasn't happening. She'd made it clear, long ago, that I couldn't say anything about it to her. On only one occasion – we were living in Pretoria then and perhaps being in civilization had brought her back to her senses, or perhaps the extent of the violence scared her – but on this one occasion she couldn't but be completely aware of what was going on. He was like a wild animal, screaming and beating me with a cane with a round silver knob. He couldn't seem to stop. I think that this incident scared even him, because he checked my body in the morning, pulling off the sheet and looking at the damage without a word.

I asked her about this when she was safely living in England: why had she done nothing? She said she was sorry, just as she was sorry about the Goedgegun ordeal, but she'd had no choice. She felt I should understand that, and indeed I did. She told me that on that last time, in Pretoria, she'd threatened to leave him because it was that bad. She wanted me to feel sorry for her and of course I did.

It was during this time, in Gabs, when we thought we might be going back to England, that I began to spend a lot of my time in the kitchen with Mpanda, our cook. I was interested in the knives he used, one in particular – a meat knife with a beautiful, chiselled end. It was probably only eight inches long, but it was very strong and sharp, perfectly honed and lovely, made supple and ingenious with use. Mpanda liked to sharpen it on the edge of the cement step leading down from the back door of the kitchen on to the bit of scraped earth where the servants gathered, laughing and drinking tea. This piece of scuffed earth had become smooth as concrete. Mpanda, after using the step to do the initial sharpening, would finely hone the edge on the hard bare earth, spitting on the blade from time to time. As he rubbed the edge of the meat knife across the surface, it made a noise that grated on my nerves. Stop that, I yelled. What is bothering you now? he demanded. Everything is bothering you, missy, I think the spooks are after you. He scraped more softly and then ran his calloused finger over the edge and when he was done, I took the knife from him and ran its edge along my lily-white finger. But I spent altogether too much time with the knife and Mpanda got suspicious. His eyes cut my way one morning and he said, It's enough now playing with this knife, missy, leave it be, this knife needs to be by itself again. He seemed to be saying, don't, and I became terrified that he'd divined what was in my heart.

I kept away from the kitchen and from Mpanda after that. I felt that he was on to me, and besides, he had every reason to recognize my intent. He'd just had a nasty set-to with my father himself, over some minor matter, but of course it had escalated into an ugly scene. I'd watched it all happen from under cover of the lemon trees just beyond the defunct outside lavatory that was my private clubhouse. Mpanda was walking away from the house, heading swiftly for his quarters at the bottom of the garden. He looked upset. My father materialized out of nowhere the way only he could, slamming the screen door behind him. Mpanda stopped and turned for an instant and my father delivered a furious kick that reached the top of Mpanda's thigh, close to his groin, and sent him reeling. For a moment the black man lunged at the air as if to grab hold of it before he hit the scuffed earth, his fist breaking into an open hand that skinned the surface as he fell. I wanted to run to help him up, but of course I was frozen, and of course my father was standing there screaming insults, threatening to fire the only cook that had ever lasted more than a few months in our miserable household. It was Mpanda's face that hooked me. It was the way his jaw moved and it was his look of barely concealed rage, of pent-up fury that chilled me to the bone. He was just waiting for a chance to get back at that tyrant, that dog; he was waiting for the time to come. Something broke loose in me and it set off a raging in my blood. I couldn't breathe and my body had turned to rock. I was waiting for my father to make a single move – I was willing him to do it – and my body would have lunged across the static that separated us and hurled him to the ground.

Staring down at the man at his feet, my father could quite easily have put his boot on the soft wool head, and it looked as if he would, but then he lost interest, and it seemed as if he were merely loitering out there in the garden, waiting for something new to happen so he could send his instinctive force out to crush it. I was shivering, but I knew that the magic had moved. My father was in a dream of his own making, dissociated, absent. Seeing him that way made me feel that it was utterly possible to stick a knife in him. Perhaps he wouldn't notice until it was too late. Perhaps he wouldn't even see me until it was done.

Mpanda had disappeared into the haze, his trousers flapping in the wind, his body rocking in the glare. My father had vanished too. There was only me left. I looked for the knife, as if it might somehow be lying there on the sharpening ground, but it wasn't. I found it in the drawer in the kitchen, lying peacefully with the other knives. I picked it up and felt its weight. I made a short slice on the inside of my wrist and saw the blood bubble up. Didn't feel a thing. I put the knife back in its place and waited for nightfall, when it wouldn't be missed.

That evening I hung around the kitchen as Mpanda made dinner. Do your homework, he said, using my knife to cut through the beef. Don't be messing in here. He was making stew and had already sliced the onions. I don't have any homework, I said. He was surly, dark within himself, not wanting me to be around him. He smelled bad. His skin, usually shiny and dark as wine, had lost its lustre, his brown eyes were empty. I'd already tried to cheer him up by giving him two whole cigarettes from the round tin of Capstans, but he wouldn't even look at them. Oh, go on, I said, take one; you know you want to. He ignored me, running his finger under his nose, turning his back on the cigarettes.

No one said much at dinner that night. My father tried

to force some mental arithmetic at me, jabbing out a long list of numbers I was supposed to add together in two seconds, the way he could. I can't even remember the numbers, I said. Well, I'll repeat them for you, he said tersely, and rattled off the list again. He waited. Can't do it, eh? Not quick enough? No brain? I ignored him. My mother was getting anxious and unhappy. Susan was at the table and I could tell that she was taking a mental note, making sure that when her time came to play this game, she'd be damn sure she knew the answers. If Angela hadn't been away at school, she'd be hiding beneath her dark fringe, barely breathing. Well? he demanded, what's the answer? I was sitting on my hands, feeling the fire in my legs, not sure I could contain myself. He was enjoying himself too much to stop. Elizabeth rushed in, drying her hands on the small white apron at her waist. Quickly she gathered up the dirty plates and whisked them out of the room, then returned with a glass dish of chocolate pudding that she put in front of him, with a quick bob of her knees. Well, let's see if you're any better at subtraction, my father said, lifting his spoon and scooping the glistening pudding into his mouth. He began, 5,689 minus 987 . . . got that . . . now minus 478 . . .

I was gone. I tore off towards the bush, feeling his yells pelting my back: you bloody well get back here right this minute, you stupid bitch, or I'll thrash you within an inch of your life. I knew that my mother would be sighing. Must you? Must you? Susan would have her head down, pretending nothing was happening, looking at the chocolate pudding as if it were all she could see. But I was gone, and it seemed to me that I was flying, that I was rising up and up, high above the darkening bush, pushing on for the stars that reached out to pull me up, higher and higher, cooler and cooler, into the silence. All guilt was gone, terror had become will, and I was filled with a wild enthusiasm, a great gusto that was unquellable. I would not be my father's daughter. I could stop being his daughter by the simple act of killing him dead and not having a father: blood for blood, his blood for mine. I went farther out into the bush and I was dancing like a savage, smearing myself with dirt, stamping my feet and raising my arms to a primitive god who looked kindly on my innocence and would bless my tribal sacrifice. Then I cut that out and became a European again: I needed a certain cold whiteness to make it all come true.

I waited until it was dark when I knew that my father would have dozed off at his desk, at least for a while. I went back to the house, climbed in through the kitchen window, trampling the nasturtiums and zinnias at my feet and breathing in their sharp odours. The kitchen was quiet and spotless. I looked in the fridge and ate the rest of the chocolate pudding. I went to the drawer and took out my knife. I thought for a minute that the knife was vibrating, but no, that was me. I heard the soft voice of the fridge warning me to keep calm, stay deadly.

The knife started out lying down the side of my bed,

inside the sheet, sleeping against my thigh. I didn't want to touch it. Now that it was out of its natural place, its coldness was snaky and repellent, but slowly the steel warmed until it reached blood temperature, and then it seemed part of me, all of one piece. Then I was the knife and it was me. I wanted it red and glowing to keep myself stoked, on fire, and to make its purpose refined and pure. They did that when they branded the cattle, the iron was red, and the clippers when they castrated the bulls, the steel was scarlet. I had to keep thinking all the time to keep out the fear. How would I even be able to locate a heart like his, let alone shove a knife in deep enough to make him stop? As I waited in the darkness, I saw him as a rogue elephant, trampling the bush, tearing up trees in his path. Night after night I waited with the knife in my hand. Night after night in the soft glow of my night-light, I waited for the house to lie down in darkness.

When he came, I had to be fully present to be able to think and act; there was no other way to pull it off. I forced myself to stay alert, waiting, and that is why I have always remembered that night. On the other nights, the imperative was to wall off, to disappear and not remember. The only light was the moonlight; it came through the window overlooking the garden with the Union Jack flying. It washed over my bed and anointed me as I lay there, preparing to slay a god. I heard his feet walking down the corridor, step by step. I was counting, one to fifteen, holding each number in my mind, to keep from entering a trance. When my door opened, and he was there, I concentrated not on the dark shadow, but on the gold moonlight that was flooding the little covered porch beyond my door, so when it opened, quickly, I saw the gold. It nearly snagged me. I found myself entering it, becoming one with it, but I could stop myself from dissolving because the knife was right there in my hand, and I was the knife, and it was me. When he reached my bed, I knew instantly that he would grab my pillow and shove it over my face. But before he could, I rose up, springing to attention like a Gurkha, my arm raised as I lifted the knife high in the air to bring it down deep into his heart. It was a moment of great beauty. I saw my hand descend, as there he stood, his eyes held, transfixed, green, the colour of mine. The knife came down, but it was so brief, the beauty, before the knife was knocked, and I with it, sideways into the sheets. I tried to scrabble for it, found it, and was about to grab it back and up again. But he tossed me sideways. A hand rammed into my face as my nose broke into blood. Mine not his.

When I knew that he wasn't dead, and that I wasn't dead, in that moment I felt the deepest despair. I should have known that he'd be unkillable. I should have known. Only now it was worse, now I was the killer. I'd become him. Just trying was enough to damn me, I knew that, it was the thought as much as the deed, the attempt as much as the failure. I was lost. I was far, far beyond God's mercy, lost in the jungle of cobras. Nothing could save me now.

Eleven

WE WERE MOVED NOT TO ENGLAND, BUT TO MAFEKING. The excitement died down. All that talk about pulling out of the colonies proved to have been a false alarm. We were to stay on, for Queen and Country, keeping the colonies going a little longer. In those last days in Gabs, after my attempt to kill him, my father and I didn't look at one another, but life went on, and we continued the same as before, as if nothing had happened. Almost. We sat at meals the way we'd always done: please pass the salt, can you hand the butter, may I leave the table now? We had the routine down pat. But he cut out the mental arithmetic and sometimes he came home very late, and when he did, the servants waited up for him and served him dinner alone. There was a different atmosphere in the house. My mother had retreated beyond the mosquito net and her retreat seemed final. She barely looked at me. The two of them lived in a stiff silence and said barely a word to one another. It was as if we all knew now, without the shadow of a doubt. The old game of pretending couldn't really go on in the same way and as a result we shunned one another like the plague.

The knife had disappeared and Mpanda asked me for an explanation. I said, truthfully, that I had no idea where it was. I remembered that night, but the details were breaking up in my mind, scattering, leaving bits all over the place that I tried not to trip over. What remained with great clarity was the knife itself, and the act of raising it in order to kill. Slowly, my act of vengeance, my attempt at cleansing, became ugly and dirty, and it became hidden like the knife – almost forgotten, but not quite. Like everything else. And then the knife, from its half-remembered place, began to hunt me down. I saw it everywhere – in every glint of sunlight, in the radiance of the setting sun, even in the thin moon that had straightened itself into an icy tip that pointed accusingly at me. It was only a matter of time till the knife and I would join again and be one.

I was turning into a ghost. Confusion had set in, memory had cracked and in the mirror when I saw my face I seemed not to know quite who I was, or what I'd done. Sometimes I woke screaming, with my head full of terrifying images: a featureless face staring at me in the darkness, a child drowning in feathers, my mouth full of scorpions and slime, and when I awoke, my sheets were so coiled that it looked like I'd tried to strangle myself.

My father was doing no better. By the time we reached Mafeking, he must have known that there were only a few more years of Africa left to him. England was going out of business in the colonies. Our overseas possessions were soon to be handed back, and that made him redundant, out of a job. He'd never stepped inside a public school and had in any case no interest in the Etonian ideals of fair play, good form and honour. He was in opposition to all those illusions because he lived by the tactics of the Sinn Feiners. And so, with no private money to fall back on, and with no qualifications except those of a civil servant from a defunct empire, he had nowhere to go except England, the country that had brutalized the Ireland of his youth.

He was flailing about like a maimed whale, hiding out from the future. We'd lost the furious connection that had once bound us so tightly together. He was as far out as I was. I can barely remember him from those days. He'd forgotten all about me. He was fighting it out with himself now. He seemed to know that he was doomed. England's time was up and his time was too. I smelled his suffering far off on the wind, but I had no pity for him. I wished to hell that he'd never jerked me into life.

Mafeking recognized my need for punishment and took me on. The first ordeal was school. Angela, having refused to submit to the holy women of the convent in Mafeking, had been expelled. She was now at St Mary's in Johannesburg, with Myfanwy and Vyvyan le Cordeur. I was still at home, and home was now Mafeking. The convent was where the English girls went but, because of Angela's expulsion, obviously I couldn't go there. Instead I was put in the public school, where the Afrikaners went. Since the time of the Boer War, Mafeking had been divided on ethnic lines much the way Belfast is. After Mafeking fell in 1902, the Boers had been herded into what were to be the first concentration camps and many of them had suffered and died there. Mafeking had forgotten none of this, and the public-school kids were happy to take their revenge on any stray Brit who entered their laager. I was easy prey.

In the Mafeking public school, girls wore tunics of dark green. These tunics were worn with a shirt and tie and had wide pleats that fell from the yoke to the knees. I inherited, as usual, Angela's schoolgirl's tunic from the convent, but it was pale not dark green: the tunic wouldn't take the dye that was used on it and it remained stubbornly pale – announcing my origins to the whole school. I was dead meat, if not by my accent, then by the paleness of my tunic. I was the enemy, and at every lunch break I'd be shoved into a circle with a large brute and made to fight him. In time I got better at it, but the cruelties of the place were too much for me. By now, I'd lost my nerve. My warrior days were over. I was barely able to keep my head above water, and it soon became clear to me that it might be better not to bother. I had two near-misses on my bicycle, once colliding with the wheel of a car, once riding across the railway line too close to the approach of a speeding train. People screamed at me out of car windows, pointing fingers at their heads to indicate that I was sick in the head. I never once mentioned these incidents. I had a sense that I was trying to do myself in, but I couldn't stop.

In Mafeking we lived in a place called the Imperial Reserve. At that time, colonial expats were still living in compounds with glorious names. The Imperial Reserve was not much more than a scruffy, dirt-tracked collection of prefabs and older houses, some with well-established gardens, others surrounded by a square of dust and a willow or acacia tree and a few red geraniums planted inside the rim of a tyre. Our house was easily the nicest house in the Imperial Reserve, but it was also the house where a horrible accident had happened. It was large and cool, and it had some of the elegance of the older houses. The front of the house had a long, screened-in porch, with a red-tiled floor that was polished every morning; there were lots of trees to shade the rooms, and I had a bedroom at the back of the house, close to the kitchen and the backyard. The backyard was where the accident had taken place. Everyone knew the story, and within days of arriving at the Reserve, we'd been told all the details.

There was a rose garden and a pond full of scarlet and orange goldfish, with small irises planted on the rim of the pond. A woman who lived next door gave us drawing lessons and I liked the way the shape of the red-hot poker could be reproduced so accurately on a piece of paper. This quiet house was a haven from the rest of brutish Mafeking, but it couldn't prevent the slide that had begun in my head.

I'd heard the story about the boy who had been digging in the dirt of the backyard when a bomb, unexploded since the time of the Boer War, had gone off in his face, blinding him and blowing his arm to bits. I wanted to know exactly, precisely, where it had happened. It was close to the wire fence, not far from the old well, and across from the tree where the rope and tyre hung. I spent a great deal of my time there, morbidly imagining the scene. Quite close to us on the Reserve lived a crazy colonel, who was suffering from shell shock. He had a reputation for being trigger-happy, and anyone of right mind kept away from him. As soon as I heard this, I began creeping out late at night with a bag full of stones, which I'd toss on to the colonel's roof and then run back into the bushes close to his house. He'd come flying out with his shotgun loaded and fire straight at me into the darkness, thinking perhaps that the troubles had begun, or that the old troubles had returned – I never knew which. I felt the quick breeze of the bullet close to my cheek and went home quietly to bed.

Soon my behaviour was getting to be just as crazy as the colonel's. I'd taken to jumping from the roof of one servant's quarters to the next. There was quite a big gap in between and the risk intoxicated me; it helped me feel alive, on top of things. Then, for some reason that I wasn't told, we were asked to move out of the nice big house and were installed instead in an ugly prefabricated horror across the way. Someone more important must have needed our house on the Imperial Reserve. It was a bad sign: things were slipping for my father. At school, things were getting a bit better for me. I'd begun to put up a good fight in the playground and now I could really hurt people. There was a nice teacher who had some idea of my difficulties and did what he could, and there was a boy, Norman, who, in the quietest way, came to my defence in the classroom, on those awful occasions when the teacher was out of the room and ink pellets came flying through the air, along with grasshoppers, lizards and frogs, which, after stones, were the best ammunition for slingshots.

Now that we were in the Republic, which was pumping out gold and diamonds like there was no tomorrow, there were real shops for my mother, not too far away. And we could drive through South Africa to the coast and spend a holiday at Durban, and swim in the sea. We could go to the Kruger National Park and try to catch sight of wild animals through our car windows, rather than hoping to God that none were lurking around in the backyard. We could buy clothes rather than having them made. The main street in Mafeking, which my mother turned her nose up at, provided a very different shopping experience from what we were used to. There was a hairdresser with a trained person inside it to do the Toni perm – not some jaapy woman in the bush who left the hair all frizzy and coarse. There was Barclays Bank, of course, but there was also the Standard Bank, and a proper police station and a jail and a courthouse. There was a chemist and a stationery store, a barber and an ice-cream parlour, a café or two, a restaurant, a haberdasher, some clothes and shoe shops. There were street lights and traffic lights, and the roads, rather than following prehistoric tracks, were laid out on lines more human than we were used to. The roads had names and one road led into another, and if you headed off in a certain direction, there was a reasonable chance that you could get back to where you started. There were butchers and bakers and grocery stores and hotels and bars, and even a toy store where I could buy cheap pearl necklaces when I'd saved up enough. Oh, in Mafeking there was everything you could dream of. And a hospital that wouldn't kill you if you had to go there, but of course if it was very serious you had to go to Jo'burg or Cape Town. There were Slegs Vir Blankes (Whites Only) signs everywhere. We didn't have those in the B.P. because there it was understood.

The trips inside South Africa, to the sea or the game reserves, were welcome reprieves, but I had to go back to school and it all started up again. Riding home to the Imperial Reserve, I would be waylaid by close-cropped blond delinquents, who'd push me off my bike, knock me around and threaten to cut me up if I told. They didn't have to press the point: it was a threat I'd understood long ago. These attacks were a daily occurrence. They'd take place just beyond the railway tracks, before I reached the safety of the British part of town. In the midst of all this, teetering on the edge of adolescence, barely able to keep going, Norman turned up. One day, when I was in the midst of my troubles with the hoodlums, there he was. He rode up, took one look at the situation, put his bike down carefully on the ground and, without a word, beat the living daylights out of my tormentors. Then he rode off without even a glance in my direction.

Norman was a bit older than I was. He was an Afrikaner, tall and blond with a nice face and body. He was quiet and thoughtful and he hung out with two other boys who were much more noisy than he was, and when they were jumping over desks, or shouting obscenities out of windows, he'd just smile. He sat at the back of the class and I sat near the front. He didn't speak to me, or I to him. I knew nothing about him at all, and yet every day as I got my bike out of the rack near the toilets – where a child had died having an asthma attack – I'd see him get his bike and push it slowly towards the school gates. I would do the same, but once we were out of the gates, we would head in different directions and I'd step into one of my terrible panics. It was like hitting a minefield. I couldn't move, couldn't leave the safe spot where I'd last seen him. Eventually, of course, I'd have to get moving, riding through a quiet part of town, past the café and the Indian stores and garages and then down the main street with all the big buildings and the wide awnings to keep the sun off the nice things inside the shop windows.

But after the main street and the stores, in that dangerous stretch just after the railway line, I would feel the panic rising again and do my best to conquer it as my head flipped right and left, left and right, on the lookout for my attackers. But they didn't come back. Days went by and no sign of them. I didn't dare to hope, but then a week passed and there was still no sign of them. It was only when I got a puncture and got off my bike that I happened to see, riding along nonchalantly behind me, about sixty yards back, Norman. When I got to the fence that enclosed the Imperial Reserve, I turned back again and, astonishingly, he was still there. I lifted my arm to give him a wave, and he ducked his head and turned to go all the way back to his part of town.

We never said anything about this, of course not. But after that I didn't so much mind going to school. Sometimes when a gob of spit landed on the back of my head I would turn up my nose, as if it were nothing. I was having long conversations with Norman all day long in my head, and before I went to sleep a picture of his face would come to my mind. He was always smiling. Sometimes his head would duck upwards in that little signal he'd given me that day when I got a puncture and he left me at the gates, home free. He and I talked a lot, slowly and deliberately, in Afrikaans, in an ordinary way, all within the safety of my mind. And, as time passed, he became a more fully formed fantasy: he'd tell me that his father worked on the railway and that he had a little brother who annoyed him and a mother who liked to cook milk tarts and koeksisters and that I should come round to his house one day and try some. And all this time he and I never exchanged a single word.

Apart from Norman, there was one other consolation in Mafeking and that was riding my bike as far away from the Reserve as I could. Sometimes I'd stop at the house of a woman I'd met somewhere and have some orange squash. We'd sit on the stoep for a moment together and she'd ask me to tell her about school. I told her wonderful stories about what was happening at school, about the grapes we got and the peaches, and about what a good person Meneer was and how I was learning about Jan van Riebeeck, again, and about the Dutch East India Company and the early settlement of the Cape, again, and the Voortrekkers, again, and how the Union of South Africa came to be. I never once mentioned Norman. Once I went in to wash my hands and I saw on the mantelpiece a little, crunched-up baby's shoe, complete with laces, all preserved in brass. I asked her who it had belonged to because clearly it had been well worn, and she said it had belonged to the baby who'd died. I never went back.

After that, I took a different track when I went down to the stream of brown water with weeping willows at the end of the town. I'd sit in the shade and eat Marmite or peanut-butter sandwiches that Mpanda had made me from wonderful store-bought bread that was thick and solid and didn't have a single hole in it, nor a blackened crust, nor cracks down the middle. He cut fat wedges and wrapped the sandwiches up in greaseproof paper, and he asked me to keep the paper and bring it back so he could use it again.

Sometimes we were allowed to make fudge or toffee

together in his kitchen, but Mpanda soon took over the whole thing because I was so clumsy and accident-prone. Burns from either of these could be terrible because of the sugar content, which was pretty much all there was with either toffee or fudge. He said that it could give as bad a burn as tar, and he wouldn't let me near the stove. He shook his head at my cuts and bruises and would get quite annoyed with me. What is the meaning of all this hurting, missy, why all time falling down and breaking bones? You should be in charge of yourself better by now. When I was your age, in Nyasaland, I was in charge of a whole herd of goats and three cows. No bad thing happened to any one of them. You have only your one self to take care of and you are doing a very bad job.

At night, visitors sometimes came and had drinks and dinner at our house. They would park their cars, big American Chevys, or sometimes a Cadillac, on the dirt road, which was corrugated and tough on cars. We had a Chevrolet too, our second, but we didn't have a driver in Mafeking the way we had in Gabs. People were driving all over the place by now, everyone we knew had a car, and even women were driving. But not my mother, of course. She wouldn't have dared to show my father up in that way. I don't know quite when she did learn to drive, but she remained all her life a nervous driver, sitting up straight and peering anxiously out of the window, as if there were something dreadful up ahead, braking at the wrong moment, and making me nervous when I was in a car with her. I of course found myself driving in precisely this kind of way when it was my turn to get behind the wheel.

The Chevys of the time were just beautiful, with their voluptuous shapes and wide rumps, their oversized wheels, and the deep comfort of their suspension. They had a smell unlike anything else and it promised wealth, open roads and freedom. Sitting in the back seat with my sisters, I would stare out the window as the outside sped by, and I'd imagine that my father was the chauffeur and that, instead of driving us where he wanted to go, I would order him to take us to a nice shady house, or the beach, or anywhere that was miles away from Mafeking. When we had visitors, I would get inside the soft, shiny seats of the visitors' cars and run my fingers down the seams, rolling the windows up and down, looking out at the night and listening to the insects in the trees. Sometimes I sat in the driver's seat and thought of driving away. I'd learned how to drive a tractor on the farm and I didn't think that a car could be that different, but the voices inside the house stopped me from trying. One night, I stood behind a tree as my parents came out to wish their guests good night. I knew that once the guests were on their way, my parents would tear them to shreds. My mother would start. Did you see her hair, and the colour of those shoes? She's really let herself go since she's been out. My father: the man's a bloody fool. Can't imagine how he manages to be head of the police. I don't know why he thinks he knows anything about the B.P. when he's barely spent a year here. And all this rubbish about independence. I'm sick to death of it.

The guests got into their car; the man lit up a cigarette and started the engine. In a flash, without even thinking about it, I found myself round the back of the car, sitting on the wide bumper, hanging on as the car pulled out and started off down the road. As the car picked up speed, I'd hang on for dear life but pretty soon I just couldn't and I'd want to jump off, but didn't know when was the best moment, so often as not I'd still be hanging on by the time the car was going too fast for me to jump. Then I'd have to because I was getting to be too far from home. I'd be dragged and my legs would be ripped up on the gravel road. Once I tipped forward and fell flat on my face and I was scared to go to breakfast in the morning because there were bits of gravel stuck in my face. Mpanda, clucking his tongue and sighing with sadness, picked the pieces of stone out of my face with some tweezers he'd boiled up in a saucepan.

I looked such a sight that even my mother knew that something was wrong with me. Sometimes she would come into my bedroom where I sat cross-legged on my bed, staring into space. She'd try to get me to talk, asking me what was the matter. Why was I always sulking? Why was I so miserable and unhappy? What was the matter with me? I didn't answer her; it was as if she wasn't there. Sometimes I would lie back on my bed and close my eyes and pretend I was sleeping. She'd be left sitting there in the silence. Payback time. I kept it going until she left me in peace. But she was exasperated and impatient and worried too. I wasn't going to snap out of it. Something would have to be done.

Boarding school is often the British solution in situations like these. Angela had been at St Mary's in Johannesburg for a year or so, and the le Cordeur girls were still there too. I was informed that I would go there at the beginning of the year, when I was thirteen. My spirits were so derelict that I'm not sure I could respond much, but something told me that the worst was over. I'd be getting out of the house. Starting afresh. I could begin again and nobody would know anything about me, or the things I'd done. Angela came home with her school trunk and fished out anything that was too small for her and gave it to me. The summer dresses were pretty, blue and white, a small floral print, and at St Mary's they wore skirts and not tunics in the winter, with the usual shirts and ties and a purple blazer and lace-up shoes. Angela, after she'd given me everything she didn't want, sat me right down. She told me that she had a good reputation at St Mary's and that she was intending to be made into a prefect. It was a highly prized position and not easy to come by. I was not – repeat not – to mess things up for her when I got there by being a crybaby, or a wreck, or by flying into one of my panics out of nowhere. The nuns were very strict and they wouldn't put up with any nonsense from me. She'd been talking to Mummy, she said, and apparently my behaviour had been very odd and she didn't want any of that going on at St Mary's. She was respected; it was the only school she'd really been happy at and she did not – repeat not – want me to come in and ruin everything for her. Nor did she want to be responsible for me there. I was thirteen and I'd have to just get on with it. She would show me how to sew on my name-tapes and help me pack my trunk and then that was it, finished and klaar. Klaar means the same as finished – it's repeated, to make the point.

We were packed off on the train with the other kids coming down from Dar es Salaam and Mombasa, and from Bulawayo and Salisbury and out-of-the-way places that had no good schools of their own. We stayed on the train for two nights, breathing in the soot as we hung out of the windows, shouting at boys, who were more often than not travelling up to St John's, our brother school in Jo'burg. We created nuisances of ourselves in the dining car, rushing up and down the corridors and banging on people's doors, screaming as we stood on the galloping bit between the carriages, where it seemed certain we'd fall through. Ange got her period for the first time on the train and was crunched up on the top berth in agonies, completely out of action for most of the trip. I was beginning to enjoy myself. It was wonderful to lean out of the windows as far as you could and see the smoke blowing back at you. All our crevices were black by the time we got there, in spite of the amenity of a small, cramped shower that you had to line up for. The stewards came round and turned down our sheets at night, and they were so young that we had a good time with them, and took puffs of their cigarettes. A whole new world was opening to me. I could see it out there as the land whizzed by and we stopped at little stations along the way and watched the piccanins jumping up and down outside our windows, asking for pennies. At night, the rhythm of the train was soothing, as was the smell of polished brass. The rails clicked and doors slammed loudly in the middle of the night or in the early morning when the train made stops to pick up passengers. Lying in your berth you would hear hurried Afrikaans voices urging passengers to get on the train quick, quick. It was romantic and exciting. I was speeding along to a new destination, to a new future. No one knew what a wet blanket I was, or what had happened to me. On the train, no one seemed to be picking on me, or throwing my things out of the windows. I was free. I could begin again. I could be a new person. I was going to the City of Gold. Everything bad was over, finished and klaar.

Twelve

OF COURSE, ANGELA WAS RIGHT TO BE APPREHENSIVE AND
I turned out to be a real liability, particularly in the first
weeks when I could barely function. The whole place with
its order and regularity was beyond my comprehension.
The bells sounded out what we were supposed to do every
hour and minute, and so much time was spent on our knees
in the chapel, wearing veils that were tied with ribbons that
cut into the back of our ears and turned them bright pink.
I couldn't get used to it. Under my desk or pew I'd secretly
shed my lace-up shoes and set my feet free, as if I was back
in the bush. I'd squirm in clothes that were unfamiliar and
stiff, and wearing nylons on Sundays was an ordeal. They
pooled at your knees or ankles and the suspender belt sliced
into your waist when you walked. And all those people –
lines and lines of girls shoving and pushing to grab as many
sandwiches as they could under the trees at the morning

break. Tables were laid out and whoever could snatch the most was getting it right. I was bewildered and alarmed by everything and everyone. People ran instead of walked, except when a nun came into view, in which case they'd brake and begin to walk demurely. Every moment they knew what to do and how to do it. These were cool and sophisticated schoolgirls, very familiar with one another and the procedures of school, and very curt with new girls. They had big tuck boxes full of extravagant sweets and Swiss chocolate called Toblerone in a box shaped like the Alps. They had money and class and plenty of clothes and they looked at me the way my mother did – like something that had been dragged in backwards from the bush.

Angela was called in to sort out one emergency after another. She'd turn up in my dorm where I was sitting on my bed behind drawn curtains, refusing to move. With her hands on her hips she'd demand: What is it now?

I need a bra.

You do not.

I do.

You have nothing to put in a bra.

I still need one. Everyone has one.

You can't. Mummy wouldn't allow it.

I have to have one or I'll get killed.

Will you stop being so melodramatic! Okay, Okay. Don't start. I'll see what I can find. Now shut up and get out of here and go to swimming, which is where you're supposed to be right now.

Of course swimming was the one place I could absolutely not go because that would be announcing to the whole swimming hut and therefore to the entire school that I did not own a bra.

After a few weeks of being a drip, and of snivelling and whining, I had an epiphany. It happened one afternoon as I saw the precise nature of the power structure in my form. My old friend Vyvyan le Cordeur, who had been at the school from presumably the moment her eyes opened, was in charge. No one questioned her authority; she was it. She had a lapdog friend called Penny who obeyed her every command; the two of them had been in this symbiotic connection from the time they'd arrived at St Mary's at the age of six. Penny had long plaits down to her waist like Vyvyan's, except hers were very dark brown, almost black, and Vyvyan's were gold. Penny was thin and sallow-skinned. Her hair was pulled back from her forehead and had been for so long that, what with the weight of her braids, her hairline was receding. People wondered some-times if she had a touch of Indian blood, but no one said anything out loud. Penny was an only child, spoiled rotten, and she was devoted to Vyvyan. The two of them walked around as one, and Vyvyan made decisions about every-thing without consultation of any kind. Vyvyan ruled.

It was clear what had to be done. I had to break her: it was the only way I knew how to stay alive at St Mary's. It was the only way I could make certain that Mafeking was not repeated in Johannesburg. Memory draws a kindly haze over the details of Vyvyan's dethronement, but within a short while, I'd toppled her. I then became a bully, making sure, by foul means, that I had everyone under control. My real coup was stealing Penny – getting her to throw Vyvyan over the side. Penny could see where things were going and within a short period of time her allegiance shifted. Now she was my best friend. Vyvyan's downfall was complete. After that I hit my stride. A few studious and less rebellious girls moved off into a different pack, forming a splinter group run by Kim Theron. The girls in my gang, whether they knew it or not, were headed for trouble. I had no qualms about this military-style coup. I'd learned survival in the bush: kill or be killed.

St Mary's was an Anglican girls' school that took boarders and daygirls. It was High Church, run by an order of nuns from Wantage in England, but there were also teachers who came in from the outside who were normal women. The daybugs were scum, of course, and we didn't give them the time of day, unless, like Lesley Barker, they had things to offer. Lesley let us use her house for parties at half-term. These were wildly exciting events that we planned to the last detail from the very first day of term. I went home with Lesley on those Sundays when we were let out, and for weekends, and I got a glimpse of how other households operated. On Sundays we got into Lesley's dad's car, threw off our felt hats and stripped off our white Sunday dresses, stockings and lace-up shoes and, right then and there, put on shorts and flip-flops, wriggling around in the back seat so we wouldn't be seen taking off our clothes as we were being driven along a beautifully manicured Waverly street.

I was in a new world. St Mary's was a real school. It had expensive fees and generous grants and endowments. It had beautifully maintained gardens, hockey pitches, tennis courts and a swimming pool. People went in for galas and competed with other schools at hockey and tennis. We heard opera and went to plays. We had a huge auditorium where we put on our own plays and concerts. The classrooms had wide windows and neat lines of polished desks with china inkwells. We wrote with fountain pens, in pale blue ink, and were taught to write in italic script, making beautifully curved letters, elegant as the arches in a Gothic church. There were book-lined shelves, and wooden floors that were dust-free and gleaming. Though it wasn't a convent, it had all the trappings of one and the walls were decorated accordingly: a large crucifix on the main wall, with a dead man hanging from it. His palms were bleeding, his forehead was ripped up by thorns and his heart was exposed, wearing its own smaller crown of thorns. Fortunately, I'd come across something similar in Mrs Watermeyer's house in Gabs. I'd once spent the night in her spare room and I'd had to take the picture off the wall so I could sleep. I soon got used to the gory sights at St Mary's, and besides, as with the Catholics, Mary was really the favourite and ultimately she took up more wall space than her son. Her body was never treated harshly; she wore blue and silver and was never seen without her halo, and seldom without the little man who sat on her knee.

I was astonished to find that there was a different teacher for every subject. They would come and go, changing each time a bell rang. Each subject had a number of different textbooks and we worked through them diligently to the end. There was a library, packed solid with shelves and shelves of books on every conceivable subject, all neatly classified and with not a single ripped page. There was also a lab, with long, gleaming tables, glass cases, test tubes and the occasional spread-eagled dead creature for dissection. I was amazed and enthralled by the luxuriance of this learning, by the seriousness not only of the teachers, but also of the students, and by the dazzling range of subjects to be conquered.

What astonished me about the girls at St Mary's is that they stayed in their seats until the lessons ended, put up their hands if they had a request or a question, without yelling, me, me, and were utterly prepared to be educated. I soon realized that I was not. They knew about things I'd never even heard of, and when the teachers spoke, the other girls understood what they were talking about. I could get by, or pretend to, with some of the subjects, like English or divinity or even history, but there were other things that had simply never come my way: algebra, geometry, chemistry, the solar system – I hadn't the foggiest. I was taken aside by teachers who wanted to know what I had learned so far. They started with the languages and that was easy enough, no Greek, no Latin, no French. Oh dear. I threw in my one success. Afrikaans? Well, yes, that was all right, Miss Grant supposed, reminding herself that it was an obligatory language, but Afrikaans, she told me firmly, was a bastard language, not a true tongue. Then we got to the really hard bit. So how about maths? Simple equations? Graphs? All right then, what about common denominators, fractions, decimals? I don't think so, I kept saying, or maybe a bit, no, I don't think so. No, sorry, I don't know that. Too much undone here, the maths teacher said glumly, where has this child been? Let's try you out on a little simple arithmetic and see if you can catch up. A hopeless endeavour. Too much water under the bridge. No building blocks in place. This was when it first struck me that I knew absolutely nothing. It was to happen again and again. I kept coming up against momentous gaps; my ignorance was as untainted as a primitive's. If the world was round and turning, then as far as I was concerned, the flatness of the desert disproved it. When I looked at the moon I'd presumed that the cut part was missing and not in shadow. I preferred the reasoning of the Bushmen that the sun sank deep into the belly of the sand at nightfall only to be reborn in the morning, or that the moon slipped into the sea and stayed there waiting for the sun to disappear again. I simply believed what I saw and it made sense. Copernicus? Who was he?

St Mary's offered me an education, but I wasn't

interested in having it. My mind had gone its own way. I wasn't moved by the interpretations of others, and I didn't want to know how much I didn't know. Learning, when I got to it, felt to me like a matter of rote. It separated me from what was immediate and real; it numbed out sensation with its dreary repetitiveness. Reverie and reflection were all that mattered, but they had no place on the syllabus. When we were given poetry to learn by heart, I liked that, but I didn't want it explained or picked apart. I just wanted to hear and feel the rhythm and meaning of the words. Only in poetry could I find a mirror for the innermost life of the mind. And then, one day, I came across a novel. It was lying about in the dorm, and I picked it up. Olive Schreiner's *The Story of an African Farm*. I read it and I never recovered. In those pages I recognized myself. Years later, Emily Brontë's *Wuthering Heights* shook me up the same way. I knew Emily's moors the way I knew the Karoo of Olive Schreiner's African farm. I knew those emotions and the landscape that throbbed like a wild, trapped soul battering itself against the wind. I could lose myself in the voluptuous but barren landscapes, and in characters that were steeped in the elements, inseparable from the wind and rain, or the bare, scraped earth and searing sun. I think it was the idea of landscape as mind that I felt at home with, and this, combined with Schreiner's feminism, set me on fire at fifteen and woke me out of a bookless stupor.

St Mary's gave me a first bitter taste of my great

ignorance, and it stunned me. Within weeks of hitting those pristine and well-stocked classrooms, I knew I was in serious trouble. I tried to overcome my difficulty in the usual way: the less I knew, the more insolence I used to cover it. Pretty soon I was getting gated – not allowed out on Sundays – for some transgression or another. Angela would be called in to deal with my behaviour. She'd finally catch up with me hiding out at the far end of the hockey pitch and stand in front of me.

I hear you've been kicked out of the choir.

I don't mind being kicked out of the choir.

What happened this time?

I was laughing outside chapel.

How could you do that! You know we're not supposed to laugh in Lent.

I didn't think it was a sin.

Who caught you?

I.B.

Oh, God. What did she say?

She said that she couldn't imagine how I could be laughing when Our Lord was about to enter His Most Terrible Time and endure His agony on the cross and be mocked and scourged and sacrificed for the sins and follies of the whole world.

Well, that's terrific! So now we're going to be short of a contralto and you won't be able to sing in *The Passion*.

She wants me to sacrifice my voice because I've been using it lasciviously.

You've got to stop this. Right now. Or I'm going to have to write home about it.

Angela was in an impossible situation with me: she was bossy and brisk, competent and compassionate, lovable and infuriating, but she was obliged, by her assigned role as my nurse, to be always on the side of authority, whether at home or at school. So we two were constantly at odds. I'd try to behave for a day or two. And then I got caught dressing up as a nun, using two towels and a black dress to create the right effect. I was swanning around in the bathroom, everyone hooting and carrying on. And as I unhooked the lavatory chain to use it as a crucifix, Sister Agnes walked in and told me, dismally, that she was going to have to report me to I.B. Angela and I were both terrified that I was going to be expelled and we waited in terror for my summons to I.B.'s office. Her quarters faced the bowling-alley green of the quad, with, straight down the middle, the Queen's Path. This illustrious highway was reserved for nuns and prefects. The rest of us had to haul ourselves all the way round while they simply scooted down the centre. I.B.'s desk looked out over the quad, so she could see at all times what was going on in her domain.

Sister I.B. – short for Irene Benedict – was the Sister Superior, top dog after God. She was a tall, well-built nun with large bosoms, and she strode around like Darth Vader wearing a veil and crucifix. There was often a small vein pulsing in her cheek and I liked to look at it. She knew what I was doing – finding a weak spot – and it drove her crazy. As she spoke, she looked at you in a way that made you suspect that, instead of seeing a person, she was actually seeing some impediment in character or some unfortunate defect. When she had me in there, she started off in her quiet, almost conciliatory way.

I hear, my child, that you have been making mock of the holy estate, and that you have seen fit to mimic the venerable vocation of Holy Orders and make light of the Brides of Christ. I apologized and she gave a little sniff. I have been watching your progress at this school, she said ominously, and then snapped: It's customary here to lower the eyes when being spoken to. My eyes hit the ground, but before I knew it, my eyes were flying up again out of some audacity that even she couldn't crush. She sighed. I see here that we have a proud child, with a will flexed and unbroken. This is unfortunate; this makes the way very difficult. Although I am prepared to take into account, to some extent, the peculiar nature of your circumstances before you came here, you are going to have to conform to our ways or things will be very hard for you. Is that clear? I nodded vehemently, trying to keep my eyes on the ground. It is not proper to pit one's small will against those who have been put in authority over us by Our Lord. She waited a while and then delivered one of her wilting speeches; she did it in the theatrical way that religious people often do. You do realize that we were reluctant to take you here, she said with pain. You are not of our church. Indeed, it would seem that you have had no experience of the discipline and order of any church, or of any form of regulation. It is so difficult to take on a child with your background, particularly at your late age – there is so much slack to gather in. But it was drawn to my attention, she said with her soft, cruel smile, that you are in need of discipline. Your father stressed that your mother felt the strain of your presence. You are a difficult child, I believe? I found myself gasping at her cold, sweet cruelty, at the shapely edge of her sarcasm. Having touched on the matter of my mother, she had rendered me miserable, my puny will snapped by shame. I was to learn from her a whole new level of sadism, perfectly honed, delicate and deadly. Hers was a real upgrade in venom and her performances left me flattened.

I.B. strode around the school with a Great Dane by her side. She swished about in her black and whites, in full regalia, the ends of her skirts picking up a fine layer of dust. She scared the bejeebers out of all of us – nuns and students alike. But as time passed, slowly I began to fall under the spell of the convent and its ways. The daily drone of the days transported me back to a beautiful barren place; the dust billowed through the window and settled on candles and flowers. It mingled with the incense and the singsong voice of the priest, sending me into a trance that would be sharply broken as two hundred hands flitted across bent faces and our voices would rattle out, Bless us, O Lord, and these Thy gifts, through Christ Our Lord, Amen. It began to dawn on me that there was a connection between the nuns' hushed and intoxicated lives and my life in the Kalahari. Something had to be created out of the tedium and only one emotion would do – passion. In the desert, the passion became disorderly and fraught, bringing people to their knees; in the convent, passion swept us along into a great ache of yearning for something beyond the self, beyond even life itself.

The nuns – or one of them in particular – a shockingly young nun from England, had just such passion. She had a soft, round face with two dimples in her cheeks and greeny-blue eyes. We imagined that she had red hair and that she was the victim of a broken romance. We used to spy on the nuns as they ghost-walked down the corridors late at night in their luminous shifts, to take a bath. We were always trying to catch a glimpse of Sister Christiana – her hair, maybe even an arm or leg – something human and of this world. The nuns weren't allowed to look in mirrors, or into any shiny surface, and we found it beyond belief that someone so young and beautiful would never look at herself again.

This young nun was to become the victim of I.B.'s wrath and severity. I.B. would give her tasks that were normally reserved for the servants, and sometimes I would find her scrubbing the chapel floor or polishing the brass and silver. It was clear that I.B. thought she was doing this to hone Sister Christiana's spirit, but the cruelty was obvious to the rest of us when we saw that Sister Christiana no longer had an amber crucifix that she'd had from her childhood. I.B.

had insisted that she give it up for God, and put away from her anything that linked her to a world that she'd vowed to forgo. Sister Christiana wasn't used to the harshness of our nuns' ways; she'd been hatched in a gentler community and at first she was bewildered by I.B.'s attempts to humiliate and censure her. I watched her as she bent her will to the life of the convent. When she knelt in prayer, her face filled up with a remote radiance; and when she was criticized or rebuked, it was as though no human emotion could touch her. Sister Christiana could make of each action a prayer and turn drudgery into devotion. There was something about this that I just couldn't understand; there was something about her love that went beyond all the bounds of normal life. Sister Christiana was besotted by Christ – it was written all over her face and it bothered me no end. How could anyone feel that kind of intoxication for a bodiless man? How could anyone have such an abundance of passion for a presence in the mind? But as I studied the young nun I wanted what she had. I was drawn to her passion and the intensity of her mind. I.B.'s insistence that suffering was the way to humility and humility the only way to Our Lord was getting to me. This little nun's ability to step over cruelty, raising her soul to a peak where it could triumph over pain and humiliation – how on earth could she pull that off? I had a backbone of steel, but mine was crippling me, whereas Sister Christiana's could transport her to heaven.

Lent provided me with what I needed: six weeks of

fasting and total immersion in prayer and penance. On Ash Wednesday, when every forehead bore its grey stigma, we began to move downwards into a charged and mysterious ritual. During Holy Week, we did a milder version of the nun's relinquishments and obeisances. In the chapel, after Palm Sunday, the statues were swathed with purple and the altar was clothed in sombre shades. On Good Friday, at the first bell, we went into retreat: twenty-four hours of silence and a complete fast. No word and no food could pass our lips. The altar was stripped bare; the Gospel of the Passion was endlessly and mournfully chanted. We virtually took up residence in the chapel and breathed in the heavy, tragic smell of incense till we were close to swooning. Those who did keel over were propped up with their heads between their knees, only to surface again and sit it out, as the minutes and hours drifted endlessly by and the procession moved silently from one Station of the Cross to the next. The desolate chime of a bell tolled out each moment of suffering; the candles were snuffed out, one by one, until we were left in misery and darkness.

During the three-hour service, I lost it. I tipped sideways and fell. My senses were on fire. The images in my head were making me lose my grip on the world. The walls of the chapel were reeling and all I could see was the whip, like a sjambok, pulling out pieces of Christ's flesh, the crown of thorns driving deep into his head, the nails entering his hands, the sword his side. I could feel his presence, taste his agony. He was there. He was there. I knew it. I believed. Nothing before had affected me so strongly, or so painfully. I was frightened because I felt so strange, and so changed. I'd lost my balance. I felt I might have lost myself.

On Easter Sunday we woke and trooped back into chapel, but now it was different; it was over. We wore white linen dresses and blue and lilac veils. We had prayers and benedictions and then, in a service of ravishing power and beauty, the veils were thrown back from the statues and ecstatic music broke out from the organ. Sister Agnes's feet trod the pedals as the chapel shook with alleluias. Father Comber, in his sparkling white robes, brought in the Paschal candle and lit it. The nuns walked in carrying tall vases of arum lilies and white roses and placed them on the altar. It was as though we'd all been holding our breath for days and now we could exhale.

All through Lent I'd been waiting to see if a gap would open in my soul through which I would see God and, though it was fleeting, no more than a glimpse, it had happened. I'd felt God's presence and I knew that he was there. At thirteen, religion gave me a taste of heaven and I hung on to it for dear life. It offered me salvation and the chance to be a good child; it promised forgiveness for the murderous rage that had threatened to kill both my father and me. Christ could deliver me from my great evil, as he'd done with Saint Augustine. Christ could help me to bury that bad child and find a new one cleansed of sin.

Now, when I thought about trying to kill my father, a great confusion covered the event. To have the idea, to wish it, that was fine, but to actually do it – to lift up my arm and bring down the knife the way I had – who could do that without being banished from humanity? I tried to move back from my murder, but I couldn't bury or forget it. It kept bobbing up like a ghost behind a curtain, and the harder I tried to repress it in my mind, the more it kept appearing in my life.

I was thirteen and in the throes of my body. I was scared rigid. I timidly tried out my new and disturbing urges at the half-term dances, but physical contact seemed to trip me into the trance-states of my childhood. Getting up close to a male body turned my body into a dead landscape that I could observe only from a distance. I told myself I wasn't ready. That was the problem. It was too soon. I needed to stay a little while longer in the chaste convent life of reverie and contemplation. I wanted to hide out in the nuns' pure world, where the body was kept firmly in check, held still by mortifications and penances. That suited me just fine.

Thirteen

BUT SO MUCH FOR ALL THAT BECAUSE THE NEXT MOMENT
I'd fallen in love. I remember the moment precisely. She
was standing on the high diving board, waiting, ready to
dive. I knew who she was, her name was Virginia, but
people called her Fudgie because she was so sweet. She was
seventeen, in her last year at school, about to matriculate
and leave to go overseas and train as a nurse. I'd seen her
face, the pale skin, the cap of brown and gold curls. Her
eyes were very blue, a bit on the small side; her gaze was
serious and steady, as if she saw a long way ahead of herself.
More than beauty, she had the face of a poet and the
demeanour of one of those women in sixteenth-century
religious paintings. But, on this day, as she stood poised on
the diving board, about to take flight, I fell as if from a
great height, and I did it watching her run on long, palely
tanned legs to the end of the board, where she made a quick

jump that sent her high into the air. Then she turned her body into a jackknife, her fingers touching her toes in midair, and held that pose an infinite second before straightening to enter the water cleanly, her head tucked between her arms.

In her black satin bathing costume and her white cap, she was as beautiful as a river bird entering the mysterious waters of the Thamalakane River. She swam gracefully to the side and pulled herself slowly up out of the pool, water cascading off her body and reflecting off the black satin. We all wore bathing costumes made of black satin, but hers was new, so the black hadn't gone rusty-brown from the chlorine. Hers was sumptuous, lying flat against her hips and belly, the contoured shape running up into a bra-cupped top with thin straps. She peeled off her white rubber cap and shook out her golden curls and laughed. Someone called her name and she turned and walked on her stork legs across the thick, green grass, holding the cap by its strap, swinging it, and then flinging herself down on her towel.

I was done for. And all at once I was so happy, so happy. And, in the next instant, miserable as sin, for how could I conceive of even saying one word to such a goddess? She was a prefect and she lived in a rarified world from which the rest of us were excluded. Prefects didn't mingle with riff-raff; they had their own common room and they kept their distance. They lived by separate rules and they had all manner of privileges. I knew that Virginia was well loved and had many admirers, I knew that, but I also knew none of them could compete with my determination to throw myself utterly at her feet. For a while, I just watched her, endlessly trying to find opportunities to go past the common room, or I'd hang out outside a classroom that she might be in, or wait outside the chapel, hoping that she'd come out, pulling the veil off her head and releasing those pent-up golden curls. Occasionally, I'd catch sight of her striding down the Queen's Path, way off in the distance, or running up the stairs to go to her dorm. I hung around the pool to see her diving or doing laps in her white cap, and I envied the water because she laid her cheek against it as she swam. When I'd had a Virginia sighting, I was ecstatic, but if I'd not seen her, not even once, in a whole day, I was inconsolable.

I wasn't the only one with such an affliction. St Mary's was awash with passionate and overblown friendships between girls who walked down to the hockey pitch, side by side, shelling the secrets of their hearts, or met in an empty classroom, or in the bathrooms late at night, so as to be able to talk with a little privacy. If you walked in on these assignations, you'd step smartly back out with an embarrassed, sorry, as if you'd intruded on nakedness. My relationship with Virginia, which at the time existed purely in my own mind, was an entirely different matter. I wouldn't tolerate it to be referred to as something as low-down and pathetic as a crush. What I felt for her I'd felt for no other and I swore I never would.

In the end, though, I had to stoop to the normal declarations. I took a little bar of Nestlé's chocolate and left it on her bed. I made sure my name was on it because I didn't want anything anonymous about this. I shouldn't have been in her dorm at all, it was against the rules and, since she wasn't even in the same wing that I was, being caught by matron would have been a big deal. Each prefect was in charge of a dorm of younger girls, who lived in two neat lines, each with curtains around a cubicle and a bed. We were allowed to draw these curtains when we were dressing or undressing, or when something terrible had happened – when the family dog died, or when a friendship came to an end. Being jilted by a girlfriend was a drama in its own right, and when a particularly long friendship came to an end, it was like divorce, with people gossiping and taking sides and, occasionally, there was an attempted suicide.

Being right there, in Virginia's dorm, standing right next to the bed she slept in, was a holy experience. I didn't open the drawers of her locker, of course not, but I saw some photos of her parents and her sister and there was a locked diary with a book of Roy Kloof's poetry on top of it. She didn't have a collection of the miniature china animals we were all collecting at the time, and she didn't have any of the holy pictures that everyone exchanged at Lent, but she did have, in a frame, a newspaper cutting of Nelson Mandela and Sisulu talking at a rally. I used her hairbrush in a quick flutter of excitement, much like the panic I felt as I lay down, flat as a corpse, for a split second on her bed, before rushing back down the corridor and stairs and out into the open air again, astonished by my bravery. And because, like all of us, Virginia was a well-brought-up girl, she wrote me a note to thank me for the chocolate. It was pinned to the messages board with my name on it and I rushed off to the lavatory to read it. I read it so many times that the folds became threadbare, and I carried it around with me everywhere I went. I still have it, and all her letters, and even a few of the rough drafts of my letters to her. In all the packing-ups and leavings, the chucking-outs, and the treks from continent to continent, I've kept Virginia's letters. Right this minute they're in the basement in a square white and gold chocolate box. Here's one of them.

Dear C,

What a beautiful little hankie, which you embroidered with your own fingers. It's too sweet. When shall I use it? When my heart is broken? On my wedding day? I shall of course invite you to my wedding. Who taught you to sew so well? It quite makes me ashamed of my own ragged little stitches.

Love, Virginia

The bit about the wedding seemed a little uncalled-for, but soon I was actually getting to talk to her a bit, in those moments after dinner, or before going up to our dorms. I would write to her in bed before lights-out, and sometimes when the dorm was in pitch darkness. We weren't supposed to have torches, because the nuns wanted to discourage reading or any other activity that might go on under the sheets. But we all kept some kind of light hidden under our beds and there was something particularly wonderful about writing to Virginia in the middle of the night, knowing she was safely asleep in her bed on the other side of the quad. Here's one of my first notes to her.

Dear Virginia,

> *I saw you sitting outside after hair washing and your hair was like pale licks of fire. Who put all the curls in like that? My hair is straight and boring as grass. You are not to be worried about the Diving Gala, of course you will win the cup. And if by some extraordinary trick you don't, I shall steal it for you.*

Love, C

The amazing thing for me about Virginia is that she liked me, she actually did. She could cut through some of my disguises and she could even discern decent qualities in me, of whose existence I was utterly unaware. Sometimes we would get the chance to talk and then I would load her up with all the things that were bothering me. She was optimistic and encouraging in a no-nonsense way that was utterly real. Oh, don't be such a damn fool, she'd say, or, where did you get such a silly idea? The notes kept coming and going. I trailed along the corridors and hung about endlessly trying to catch sight of her. I'd heard something fascinating about her: Virginia used to faint. Passed out. Just keeled over. People worried about her because of it. What would happen if she fainted at the top of the stairs? This alarmed me and I began to track her whereabouts as if, in some miraculous way, I could stop her falling, or catch her in mid-flight. The fainting was something we had in common. I knew the stage just before collapse pretty well. I often got close to it, and I felt sometimes that I had actually passed out because a piece of time was missing. It surprised me that Virginia didn't look more closely into these manifestations in the way that she would peer into other aspects of her character or behaviour. She let the fainting alone. Many years later, as a grown woman in England, she fainted and fell on to a radiator and she was badly burned on her arm. She shrugged when she told me this: you can't get through life without scars, she said, briskly, not if you're fully alive.

Virginia was fully alive and she made me aware of my own deadness. I felt it most when she wasn't around, when I was left without fantasies of seeing or being with her. But it was such a new feeling, this dependency, and I was afraid of it. In a similar way, my wild tips into depression alarmed her. She encouraged me to be dependent on myself, and she handed me the startling notion that if my happiness depended on someone else, then that person had the power to take my happiness away. The only way to be happy, she said, was to be happy inside. I'd no idea how to do this. None. I was already falling into a panic at the idea that I was going to be separated from her for a couple of weeks when the holidays came. I'd no idea how I was going to survive going home, as well as not seeing her – both prospects scared me half to death.

Dearest Virginia,

It's late at night and I'm supposed to be studying. I'm sitting on the bathroom floor, which is cold, and the room smells of baby powder and smelly feet, and I'm terrified that I'll be caught by Barrel, who's been on the prowl every night. I can't concentrate on this ruddy Maths. None of it makes any sense. I wish you were here to talk to. I keep wanting to creep into your dorm and wake you up. But I know I wouldn't if I saw you sleeping, because you've got much more important exams coming up, so I couldn't make you tired. Oh, Virginia, I can't bear it for the term to end.

All my love, C

Dearest C,

You must stop worrying about the holidays and about not seeing me. Lots of new and exciting things are going to happen to you, and you won't miss me at all. But of course I will write to you, every day. Congrats for the swimming, you did jolly well and, take it from me, if you train hard this term and next term, you could get into the Inter High gala next year. If you do, you must write and tell me, and I'll come over from England by plane with my children and watch you win the one hundred yards. I must end now as the bell's about to go.

Love, Virginia

I did survive the holidays and when I came back, Virginia began to help me clean up my act at St Mary's. She insisted that I was smart and that I should take some interest in my lessons. She encouraged me to stop getting so many order marks because I was right up there with the worst offenders. She knew about my strange ways, but she made no judgment. Not once. She sometimes asked me why I was so often infuriated and so often sad, and I had nothing to tell her. I'd hoped that by coming to St Mary's these feelings wouldn't travel with me, but they had. I'd find myself going along in a perfectly nice way and then something would annoy me, and I'd find myself smashing my friends' heads against walls, hitting them across the face, or pinning someone's arm behind their back and cranking it up as high as I could. I could just as easily force some poor wretched girl to bring a hockey stick down on my right arm to disable it sufficiently to get me out of some measly tennis match or other that didn't matter a bit. My sadomasochism was perfectly in place, learned from the master. All my destructiveness and self-destructiveness, though appalling to others, was quite natural to me. I was careful, though, to keep it under wraps, but Virginia was aware of it, and sometimes she would ask me why I did such things. I hadn't a clue.

She was also aware of the time I'd tried to kill myself. This happened just before I had to go home for the holidays. I had a terrible report card. I was not catching up at St Mary's. Teachers felt that I couldn't concentrate, that I was dreamy, endlessly slipping into my own world. I had a bad temper. I didn't like to be told what to do. I was accused of leading others astray. I knew what a report card like that would do to my father, who'd had to scrape up an education in Ireland, who'd never had the opportunity to go to university, and who thought my sisters and I were pampered beyond measure by being given the chance of a private education. As the days drew closer to the end of term, my nightly terrors mounted and the images in my head became more graphic and intrusive. I couldn't concentrate in class. My mind would begin whirring and I'd see myself way out wandering in the bush, or lying in the dark in my bed at Gabs, waiting for the generator to cut out and for the house to go black. I'd get a flash of a face that had no features, or see my mouth being crammed with feathers or snakes, or I'd see a bowl slowly filling with blood. Nightmares woke me in the middle of the night, and I'd feel certain that someone had tried to suffocate me. Just the idea of going back home made me think that I was going out of my mind. I couldn't tell Virginia. I didn't know what was happening to me, so I thought I must be going crazy. That frightened and depressed me so much that I'd find myself lying on my bed with my face to the wall, and if someone spoke to me, I'd pretend to be asleep.

I got sick. I'd had severe throat infections since I was little, but I shouldn't have had tonsillitis at this time because my tonsils had been removed the year before. But there it was: my throat swollen and red, and my fever right up. Matron, when she put the stick on my tongue and looked down there, recoiled. I was put to bed in the sickbay, and it was here that I decided it was a good time to die. I considered it carefully. My mother and father didn't love me, that was clear, so they wouldn't miss me, though maybe my mother would a little because it would make her feel bad. But, since my mother didn't seem to know or care about how much I loved her, or wanted to help her, perhaps she just didn't feel things very much and so wouldn't really miss me. I didn't want to think that she would suffer, but I'd only seen her suffer in one way, and that seemed to be because her head was filled with pain and she needed to sleep most of the time. It didn't seem likely that I could make her sad by dying when I was such a nuisance to her, and such a hateful child to my father. They would certainly be better off without me. Angela had made herself tough, so I didn't think she'd care, and, anyway, I was such a pain in the neck for her that she'd prefer not to have to worry about me all the time. If I was dead she wouldn't have to take me to the dentist on the bus because I was such an anxious nelly that I couldn't do anything like that by myself, like a normal person. But maybe she'd be sorry, and maybe my parents would wish that they'd been nicer to me, but of course by then it would be too late.

I liked the idea of the coffin. In Swaziland, when a nun at the convent died, Ange and I had gone to her funeral. She was young and beautiful, lying there, folded into the soft satin, with arum lilies tucked in around her, and one between her hands, the fingers praying so quietly all by themselves as she lay there in the garden, the sun on her face one last time. But we had to kiss her, and one of the nuns lifted me so I could reach over, and I hadn't expected that coldness, it was like when you put your hand inside the marble basin, a coldness almost watery, and so cold she was that even the sun couldn't warm her. I pulled back and the nun frowned, so I knew I'd done the wrong thing. But whenever I thought of death, I remembered the nun and it made me believe that death was beautiful, so it was quite simple really to stand on a ledge, to keep finding myself standing on a ledge, all my life, and think, shall I go?

There was Virginia, of course, but she was going away too, to England, and since I had no intention of ever going there, I wouldn't see her again either. She would be gone, like Maun was gone and the river was gone, and Violet and Elizabeth and Rena were gone. And if I was really forced to go to England, dragged there by the hair – England would kill me anyway. I'd be standing on some dirty ledge with the rain coming down, in some ugly place with the houses all on top of one another and no emptiness and space anywhere and no flatness. That was what I liked best, flatness, so that the sky could spread out and out, filling the world with a holy blue. Then I'd jump.

I wanted this time to get it right. I wanted to do one single thing perfectly. I didn't want them coming and standing round me at the bottom with that look on their faces of, do you always have to make a mess of everything? The sickbay was a good place to jump. It was at the top of the school, on the third floor, and there was a concrete path at the bottom that I'd hit. Couldn't miss really. The other time I'd jumped out of a window – pretending to be in a hurry to get to lunch – I'd only broken an arm. No, the sickbay was perfect. It was a sure thing. And when I really couldn't come up with any good reason to stay, and my mind was completely made up, I knew it was the best solution, and I said, shall I go? And the answer was yes.

Up there on the ledge no one could see me; the window faced the front of the school and few people came that way in the middle of the day. It was like sitting on top of one of the flat-topped koppies near the farm. My legs hung down over the ledge and, while I sat there, waiting to enter my trance, suddenly the beautiful blue-gum trees and the blue sky, and the heat of the sun on my body, filled me with a horrifying grief. I was so lonely out there on the ledge. I hadn't expected to feel that, or even to feel anything at all, because I was just a stick or a stone, nothing more than that. But now, on the ledge I was feeling something. I couldn't take it. I vanished instead into that place where the world became beauty and only that. I was no longer looking out of my school window. I was back in the loop of the river with water lilies pink and blue. Back where the green boat rocked among the reeds and wild duck flew, just one or two, caught up in the high, hot air that made everything so still, green-blue and everlasting. Now I wasn't so lonely there on the ledge, and I said – now – willing it, wanting to fly out into the arms of the air and be cradled there before dying.

Fourteen

BUT I WAS SAVED — YANKED BACK IN BY A LARGE LESBIAN
girl who'd come in from the other room of the sickbay and
seen me teetering there, about to take flight. She pulled me
in, but she pulled me too close to her, and I pushed her
away and whacked her across the face for her trouble. When
I was better I left the sickbay, but I almost wished I could
have just stayed there till it was time to go home. The whole
school knew, and it was a horrible feeling, a bit like having a
placard on your back, the way they did at Goedgegun: I am
a thief. I am a liar. I am a lunatic. Naturally, this incident was
regarded by I.B. as a piece of melodrama, and she managed
to be utterly shrivelling about it.

So now, she began, tucking her large hands into her black
sleeves, in your overweening pride, you have decided to take
on Our Lord's work and choose the hour of your death —
without mercy of confession, without benefit of intercessor.

She smiled her kind, chilling smile. But perhaps I give you too much credit, after all. Perhaps you are just the stupid, headstrong girl your father spoke to me about when you first came. And perhaps that moment, when you chose to challenge the authority of Our Lord, you were probably seeking no more than a little sordid limelight – a melodrama to fill out the bleakness of a lost soul far out at sea, without discipline or reverence to guide it to safe harbour. When she saw that she'd extinguished me, she suggested, quietly, as if speaking to a child she'd just tormented for her own good, please come to my office, and I will give you some readings from the Scriptures, some words agreeable to a new direction of your will. After that, I returned home to the beating that alarmed my mother sufficiently to make her threaten to leave my father.

During the end of my first year at St Mary's, and just before she was going to leave to go to England, Virginia took me home with her. I knew that she was going out on a limb; the nuns wouldn't like it and it would reflect poorly on her in some way. I was still acting up at school, still bucking authority, but I was better able to walk that fine line that kept me just within the limits of the nuns' endurance and, besides, I had chummed up with a couple of the nicer nuns and got them to have some sympathy for me. Sister Hilary, who was in charge of the choir, was particularly easy to manipulate due to a real kindness of heart, so most of the time I managed not to get kicked out. Singing had begun to make me feel happy.

Virginia had normal parents. Her father was an intelligent and thoughtful man; he may have been a writer, or an academic of some kind. Virginia often quoted him. She said to me one day that it was possible to be good without God. I found that an enormously comforting idea; it made goodness available to everyone, and it took the doom out of life. I remember having a conversation with Virginia's father about school, about what I might want to be. He was asking me questions as if I had possibilities. I was suspicious at first, thinking he was waiting to sneer at whatever I said. But he wasn't. This was a first. He told me that Virginia thought I was clever and that I would do something wonderful one day. After he said that, I didn't take in another word he said, I was so amazed. I hoarded his words in my heart for weeks and brought them out like a talisman any time I was at my wits' end.

Virginia's parents had a life that was orderly and comfortable. They didn't keep moving every six months, which my parents were now doing. Virginia had lived in the same house all her life and gone to no more than two schools, whereas I'd ratcheted up so many of both that I'd lost count. I envied Virginia's easy relationship with her father. It was astonishing to me to hear the way he spoke, and listened, to her. Above all, I could see that she loved him, simply and without torment. This made me sad. I once tried to tell her how things had been for me at home before I'd escaped to St Mary's. But it was impossible to say much about that life: the shame was too great and by now I was doing my best not to think about it. A further blurring of memory had taken place. So I merely alluded to my father's violence, and about my mother I said very little. I was loyal to her, still bound hand and foot to the idea of saving or reconstructing her, still loving her in my hopeless way: how could I not? She was my mother; I had no other. No separation from her was possible. I'd come to feel that if I abandoned her, she'd die. Even so, our connection was now so full of strain that I was glad to be at school and away from her. After the knife incident, we seemed roped together, my mother and I, by guilt and betrayal. We looked at one another, and turned away, as if we couldn't stand the look in each other's eyes.

As Virginia's last weeks at St Mary's began to whittle away, I was filling up with despair at the thought of being separated from her. I was panicking about going home too: at the end of the term I would have to go to Pretoria, since my parents, as part of the British High Commission, were moving between the two capital cities – Cape Town and Pretoria – in tandem with the South African government. These six-monthly shifts, yo-yoing between two very different South African cities, made little impression on me. I remember the seaside places in the Cape, and the jacaranda trees in Pretoria, but there's no heat to the memories and they didn't stay with me. My real life was the time I spent at St Mary's: it was the first settled home that either Angela or I had ever had. I was putting down my memories of this time in the same sacred space that I kept for the landscapes of the desert. And Virginia, of course, was ingrained on my heart.

I would gaze at her as she sat at the top of a long table, doling the starchy food we ate on to white plates and handing them to the person seated at her right who was not me. I had so little time to talk to her. Her life and mine were separated by careful boundaries. But sometimes I used to go missing for hours on end and she seemed to understand that I wanted her to come and find me. I'd be at the very end of the hockey pitch, in a kind of no-man's-land beyond the playing fields. Once I saw her walking towards me with her steady stride, her long legs cutting through the grasses. I was so dismal that I could barely lift my eyes from the ground, where I was digging into the dirt with a sharp stick. She sat down close to me.

What's the matter? she asked me. Everyone's looking for you.

I broke the stick and chucked it away. I don't know what's the matter, but it always is.

You must know, even a little.

I HATE all the time, I yelled. I just feel so angry that I want to smash everything to bits. I hit myself furiously in the face with my fist and I heard her shocked intake of breath.

Why d'you do these things to yourself? she whispered. Why do you keep hurting yourself like this? She was pained by me. I couldn't stand that. She pulled my clenched hands apart as if they were opponents, and the minute they were separated, I began to rip my nails into the eczema that crawled all over the fingers and palm of my right hand. It was raw and bloody with abuse.

It isn't your fault, she said softly, that you feel this way. Something bad must have happened to you. No one does bad things for nothing, not even murderers and rapists. They've been murdered and raped too, by someone or something. What happened to you? Who hurt you?

My mouth was crammed with feathers and snakes again and I thought I would die on the spot. I had nothing to tell her.

You have to fight back, she said, but in another way, not this way – not with violence.

For a moment she had my attention, but then my mind slipped, and I looked at the little blue flowers that covered her knees and made up the lovely shape of her St Mary's dress. A stiff blue prefect's belt nipped in her waist and caused the dress to billow out in soft pleats. Her belt wasn't all grungy and frayed like the one I had, which was cut from the same cloth as the dress and rumpled up in a minute. I saw the enamel pin at the collar of her dress; it was pale blue with a white lily arching upwards, and I remembered the school motto, *Candida Rectaque*, pure and upright. I began to rub the palm of my hand in the dirt, as if to clean it.

Stop it, she said. You have to stop it.

I thought she was angry with me, and that made me panic, but she wasn't angry. She was looking off across to where the high wire fence separated the school grounds from the outside world of houses and suburbs – the green leafy enclave of Waverly. She held my hand, dirty and all. Out there, far away from here, in the townships, she said quietly, people are changing things. People who've been hurt and beaten and murdered since we first came here to Africa. They're burning their passbooks, they're beginning to fight back.

What she said made me feel hope for the first time – that things could change, that there was an end to suffering. It was very different from the nuns' message. They told us that only suffering could sanctify us, and that we should embrace it. Virginia had said, Fight back, but without violence. She left me at the bottom of the hockey field to think about this revolutionary thought, and when I next saw her, she smiled and sent me a strange salute – a clenched fist raised in the air. It returned me all the way home, back to the bush where I'd first felt that I could be an African, a proud warrior with a spear in each hand, and the heart of an eagle. And when I left the hockey field and headed back to school, I was walking on diamonds again.

My dearest, dearest Virginia,

It's the holidays in two days, that's all I can think about. Everyone in the dorm is madly crossing off the days and pretending they're going to have the most marvellous holidays. But I'd like to break all the clocks and turn the nights back. It is more than I can think about to know that this is your very

*last year and then you'll be gone for ever. What will I do?
What will I do? I want to be brave and strong, but I don't
know if I can be that without you.*

Love, C.

Dearest C,

*I read your last letter again and again and felt so sad to be
going away. I shall miss you horribly when I go. I shall be
very miz. to leave the school and my friends, even some of the
old penguins, but you most of all. You are so much more
grown up now. I'm so proud of you, and of how brave you
were when I told you the exact day we were sailing. And you
know, I do not want to go at all now. I shall miss this house,
and, oh, how I shall miss this beautiful, beautiful South
Africa, and the sun and all our sweet servants who have
looked after me since I was so little.*

*You will be okay without me, won't you; you will be
happy? And I will come back, I promise. I must. I couldn't
live anywhere else for long. I'll come back and be a nurse in
one of the mission hospitals, and then I'll start one of my own,
a really super one for the black children, to stop all those
babies dying. And you will help me, won't you? You can be
in charge and then things will be run superbly. There, now I
feel better; now I know it is not just now that matters, but
tomorrow, later, other days that we must be preparing
ourselves for.*

So you must get a First Class Matric, my girl! Work hard,

play games well, and then you'll be a prefect. And then when
I come to Old Girls' Day in a few years, you can serve me
with watery tea and fattening cakes. And maybe you will
come to England too and we can be together again. We can
have long conversations over coffee late at night or walk
down lanes with cobbles and blackberries – and plan how our
lives shall be. And go all over Europe on boats together and
have thousands of boyfriends, but still love each other better
than all of them – until we marry, of course! And now, my
girl, you must stop having these gloomy thoughts because it's
ages before I'll be gone.

Oceans of love and a kiss on every wave!
Virginia

Virginia hung in with me after she left St Mary's and
before she went to England. She'd come and collect me
from school and take me home with her and feed me up,
but then she would take me back and leave me there without her. I thought I'd be furious and miserable when she'd
gone, but I could be a little more normal now and see things
as they were. She wrote to me almost every day and she
encouraged me to get on with my life and make other
friends. She insisted that it was the right thing to do, and a
way to keep happy and not miss her too much. But whether
she liked it or not, I was hers for keeps. She became part of
my personality; I took aspects of her and I made her part of
myself, and in this way I thought I could never lose her.

Fifteen

I HAD A YEAR LEFT AT ST MARY'S, AND IT WAS BEGINNING to dawn on me that I might have to leave Africa as Virginia had done. The talk was darkening. Now they said things like getting the hell out before it was too late. Not waiting around only to find a knife at your throat in the hand of a native who'd lived at the bottom of your yard since he was a boy. I listened to this, and as it began to mount up, it began to feel likely, and so I began to believe that I could really be taken away, put on a ship to England, and that would be it – the end of life. I knew I couldn't survive any-where but where I was. People in England would see right through me. They'd know I was a girl from the bush, a colonial, someone wild and untethered, ignorant and un-educated. How could I live among people who didn't know where I'd come from? Who wouldn't have seen the things that I knew and loved? How could I bring them the magic of the river in Maun, or of the African women walking down to the mealie fields with their babies strapped to their backs? How could I tell them how guinea fowl stepped lightly through splashes of moonlight, or describe how the scorched plains vibrated and hummed when the sun was high? What could they know of the slithery nights when the hyenas bayed at the moon and the lion gave out its solitary cry; how could they understand the underwater silence of the crocs sidling among the water-lily stems? How could I tell them any of it?

I thought I could keep Africa by making it part of me, but Africa, which had never been ours, was slipping beyond our reach. Africa was on the move now and Botswana was headed for independence. My parents were still commuting between the two South African capitals, but we were going back to Bechuanaland for one last time, when the protectorate changed its constitution and began to take steps toward freedom and self-rule. But before we went back to the B.P., we spent a short time in Basutoland (Lesotho), a tiny kingdom set in high mountains, surrounded by the Republic of South Africa. And it was in Basutoland, in my fifteenth year, that I was knocked off my feet by a boy.

It happened simply enough. I was walking along the road in Maseru one day when a small blue car with a cut-away back window – an Anglia – went roaring by and then came to a screeching halt. I, too, came to a full stop. My heart was racing and out of air. I just stared. A blond boy had turned to look back at me. Me! Wearing some ghastly skirt my mother had got me from England, and with my hair hacked off like a convict's. When I'd come back from school, my mother, as usual, had taken one look at me and got out her shears; she'd also made me scrub off the pale pink lipstick and she watched to make sure I'd removed every scrap of the pearly polish from my nails and thrown the Cutex bottle into the trash. That anyone could look at me twice was a miracle.

My mother, the makeup queen, would have no truck with us wearing makeup of any kind. That was tarty, cheap and un-English. She wouldn't even discuss it. She didn't care if every other teenager in the world was wearing pale pink lipstick and thick, clumpy black mascara; we were not going to and that was that. The one nice thing she did do on this front was to give me a pair of her shoes, black suede with little diamanté stars on the front, and I loved them. But that didn't happen much; she'd shake her head and sigh, your feet are so much wider than mine, dear, all those years walking barefoot in the bush, I'm not sure you'll ever have normal feet again. As for my father, he'd prowl around at parties, and at the occasional dance that we went to as teenagers. And, on the single occasion that we'd actually been allowed to have a party at our house, he kept barging in and switching on all the lights. We'd blink in shock and horror as the bright light irradiated the room and exposed us slow-dancing in the dark.

Before I was allowed to go out at night, he'd drag me

over to a light, fasten my chin in his fist and scrutinize my face to make sure I wasn't wearing makeup. If I was – I always was – he'd smear it across my face with his thumb. If I was wearing anything even vaguely provocative – fat chance since my mother chose my clothes – he'd make me put on something else. This was at a time everyone was wearing tight sweaters and very pointed bras, Madonna style, with stitching that went round and round into a hard cone. We wore skirts that were flamboyantly full, with layers of net petticoats, stacked tier on tier, like a wedding cake. When you spun, people could see, beneath the whirling blue or scarlet of your skirt, long beaches of golden thigh and white cotton knickers, innocent as milk.

The version of these skirts and petticoats that Angela and I wore were of course far less voluptuous. It was ordained that we never looked 'fast' – English girls were not fast. English girls did not dress in a way that drew attention to themselves or their bodies. These were my mother's pronouncements, and I don't know where she got them from, except perhaps from her women's magazines, which she read to the end of her life. But once out of the house and away from my mother's restrictions and my father's clutches, we were free and happy. Ange and I would climb on the back of a lorry that some wild boy was driving, and I'd snatch some Revlon Hot Pink out of some girl's bag and smear it on my lips, and feel just fine. We'd roar off into the night, taking over houses where the parents were away, smoking Rothmans and drinking

Castle beer. We'd hang about under the stars, or on a red-tiled stoep, winding up the gramophone so we could jive to 'Jailhouse Rock' and 'Blue Suede Shoes', or smooch around to 'Are You Lonesome Tonight?' and 'Blue Moon'. There was a lot of making-out going on all around me, but I was doing none of it. I couldn't even get to first base. Once a boy stuck his tongue into my mouth and I started gagging and scared us both half to death. The first time I felt an erection close to me I thought I was going to keel over. Once a boy knocked me over in someone's garden and lay on top of me and began to yank at my clothes and his own, but I lay there so like a stone or a twig that he stopped, and looked at me for the first time. Jeez, he said, you look like you just saw a ghost. He let me go. I couldn't have stopped him if he'd kept going, not a chance.

Angela and I were both enduring awkward adolescences, but we didn't talk about it. She had to wear some truly hideous lace-up shoes to rectify her fallen arches. My mother had also insisted that her lovely hair be permed and it ended up looking like hell; I remember her riding off on a horse in the deepest misery. I'd been forced into a leather and iron corset, to rectify a curvature of the spine. I'd got the brace in Johannesburg; some sadistic doctor thought it would straighten me out, but after some months of confinement I left the contraption on the train and waved goodbye as it sped off to Rhodesia. It was probably turned into spare parts for a tractor.

So, when I fell in love with Bruce on the road, my

reaction, so fleeting but so powerful, was alarming in its implications. I didn't know where it would lead and I didn't know how on earth I was going to manage my feelings. That blow to the solar plexus that I experienced the first time I saw him – I couldn't understand it, but it was quite different from what I'd felt for Virginia. More bodily. More scary. This boy with his blond hair and tall, slim body, though I knew him not at all – and never would – perfectly captured my fantasy of Boy. His name was Bruce Going and it was a name that suited him. He worked at Barclays Bank, but this job was far out of line with the rest of his life. He was a wild boy, addicted to fast cars and booze. At the time, of course, no one thought of anyone as an alcoholic. Bruce wouldn't even have been called a drunk: that was too seedy a term, too bottom of the barrel for someone so young. But he was well in the throes of alcoholism by the time I got to him, and he'd already had so many car accidents that his future wasn't a certainty. He wore his scars like tattoos, had ravines in his scalp and a dent in his side, where a door handle had been cut out of him. None of this bothered me a bit: I was familiar with this kind of thing. Bruce had a narrow, tragic face that I found quite beautiful. And, in spite of his wild ways, there was a quiet centre to him, a place where he could reflect, not on what he might be doing to himself, but on his future as a racing driver. I tried not to interfere with this fantasy of himself; I listened, I heard him, and I even thought he could do it.

I used to creep out at night from the hotel room I shared with Ange, and meet him at the back of the Lancer's Inn, where we were staying for our time in Basutoland. We sat in his car for hours and talked, while he smoked cigarettes and dropped them out of the car window. Being with him was risky stuff. My father had heard that Bruce was reckless and crazy, and I was forbidden to have anything to do with him, but I managed to see him most days. He took me for rides in his car up the mountain roads outside Maseru and he'd swerve in and out of the bends, getting very close to the rim of the road, racing higher and faster as we neared the top.

We were a chaste pair, Bruce and I; whatever he was doing with his body, it wasn't sexual. Speed, for both of us, was an alternative form of ecstasy. When he got behind the wheel of a car, he seemed most nearly himself, and most completely happy. His mind was immersed in speed and nothing else. He knew what he was doing, he had no fear, and he was without hesitation or doubt. He and the car were one and he was so in tune with the hum of the engine and the undulations of the road that nothing else reached him. He had perfect control and there would be a moment when things became so fast and so beautiful that in the magic of that humming speed it was almost like not breathing, and it was almost motionless. When he reached that point, he called it peaking, we entered a state of grace and everything came under the spell of beauty – the sky and the sun, the blue mountaintops and the thatched huts perched on the lower slopes, the dark trees under which Basutos sat in the shade, waiting for the bus to take them down the mountain, to town. All this filled me with a frenzy of love, not only for him, but for all that speed made visible, beautiful in its fleetingness.

We never crashed, he and I, but we came damn close once or twice. When I suggested to him that he was trying to wipe himself off the face of the earth, he laughed. I only knew him for three weeks, but something about him stayed with me, some luminous quality, something, if he could have tamed it, that might have made him the Grand Prix driver that he dreamed of becoming. He wrote to me after I went back to school, long letters in pale green envelopes with slanting handwriting. And he wrote to me when I went to England and, as time went by, slowly the letters put on length and heat. He wanted me to come back to Africa and marry him; he was learning to control his drinking and driving, or this is what he wrote. He sent me a beautiful red and black Basuto blanket and it kept me alive in the dumb, dark days in boarding school in England. He was my link to all that I'd lost and I held on to that blanket for dear life, sleeping with it every night, dreaming of going back and riding the high peaks with him by my side.

It was June 1960, the year the Congo blew – the first round of explosions that sent colonials rushing to get on boats that would get them all safely back home and away from the coming carnage. It was like India all over again:

imperialists on the run, leaving, in the places they'd conquered and the people they'd subdued, traces of the familiar, strange, sweet stench of their occupation. Something was happening in the Congo and it seemed to be something very bad. In 1960, Conrad's Congo, the land of diamonds, copper and rubber, the gem of Africa, the country of the old slave trade, had declared itself free. Patrice Lumumba, a postal worker, a revolutionary leader beloved of his people, while languishing in prison, was elected prime minister by popular vote. The independent Republic of the Congo was born. Central Africa had made herself free, free at last. There was a moment of calm, while the Belgians took counsel with the Americans to see how to deal with this. A complex web was being spun, the full implications of which would not come to light for fifteen years. At the time it seemed as if the minute this pretty country got into black hands, somehow things went wrong, and before you knew it, it was all a mess. They said it was the usual story: tribes at each other's throats, uprisings, bloody riots, strikes, conspiracies, a civil war, an army coup, a takeover, and a gruesome murder. But who was behind it all? No one knew. It was pinned, at the time, on Mobutu, a barefoot and hungry Congolese soldier who'd taken charge of the army and was, mysteriously, in possession of a million crisp white U.S. dollars.

All over the world, splashed on the front pages of the newspapers, the appalling story came out. And wouldn't you know it, Africa's heart was as dark as it had ever been, as savage as we'd all imagined. Patrice Lumumba, the great black hope, had been murdered, his body so mutilated that it couldn't be shown. Hell had broken loose in the Congo. The barbarities increased. The death toll mounted. The world looked on aghast, spellbound by the sight of so much tragedy coming out of so much hope. So this is what freedom meant to Africans? This was how they handled independence?

Meanwhile, while this was happening on the world stage, in a girls' boarding school in Johannesburg we heard the news, were riveted by it, couldn't get it out of our minds. White Christians were being killed by cannibals, the natives were on the loose, gone ape-shit, bones in their hair, paint on their bodies – wild for Belgian blood, wild for the blood of missionaries – for any blood that ran in the veins under white skin. We were terrified that the savage flood would overflow the Congo River and sweep down to the Transvaal and drown us in blood. Catholic nuns were being raped and pregnant women's stomachs slit in front of their husbands and children, the foetuses tossed up on spears. We knew the score: we were the future mothers of the white babies to come; we were the target if the future was to be black.

Glued to our radios, we heard the news. Thirty whites killed in Stanleyville, said the BBC grimly; atrocities to foreigners bound to increase; evacuation plans needed immediately. It was ghastly, we all said. Thirty whites. My God! How many blacks did you say? Well, never mind.

The men behind Mobutu and his army and police were trying to keep things in order – but what would happen to us? How far would it spread? This was the beginning of the end. At about this time, the whole school, or the boarders at least, came down with virulent dysentery, which kept us all out of class and permanently in the lavatories, lining up for a pew. Michelle Phillips said the best way was to sit on the seat and lift your legs high in the air to allow your insides to fully drain. This contagion was felt to have something to do with what was going on in the Congo – whether it was a sign of our terror, our bowels turning to water, or some deadly parasite from the jungle that had swum all the way down the mighty Congo River, through the southern tributaries, until it reached the pristine white veins of the Jo'burg water supplies – who could tell? There was frenzied terror running up and down the dormitories for weeks on end. The nuns were on edge. I.B. was in her office, drawing up a defence plan.

Then Lumumba was killed and the freedom dream died. The terror slowed down a bit after that, but it wasn't over – although it certainly was for the Congo. Elsewhere, it was just beginning. The drums began again, sending wild messages through the elephant grass and over the wide savannahs: put down the white man's burden; take back the land that is ours. These urgent messages spread like bush fire through the once quiet colonies; they wanted us out. All of us. Right now. Out. Out. Out. Finished and klaar.

Sixteen

WE WERE LEAVING. MY FATHER WAS BEING SENT BACK TO England and we went with him, my mother, my sisters and I. But before we left, Ange and I went back to the farm in Gabs one last time, and my mother came – for some reason I cannot fathom. It's hard to place her on the le Cordeur farm, since I'd always banished her from there so successfully, but she came. I was in the little room where I'd lain in the darkness with sunstroke a few years earlier, and where Rena had wiped my forehead with icy water till I could think straight again. My mother was perched on the side of my bed, as far away from me as she could get, her legs elegantly crossed. I'd entered one of my weird silent phases that she found incomprehensible and infuriating: states that when I was little were called sulking, and when I was thirty were called clinical depression. I was lying flat out on the bed, which was close to the wall, wearing shorts, my legs and feet bare. For some reason, Dan le Cordeur came in while my mother was sitting there. As soon as he was in the room, it felt cramped. There wasn't enough room or air for the three of us, and my mother and I were uncomfortable. He sat on the end of the bed, the square boulder of his body blocking out the sunlight, his hands clasped loosely between his knees. He smiled at me. Ag, shame, cheer up a bit, won't you? He moved one of his hands and rested it on my thigh. It was brown, with golden fur, and it felt heavy and soft, warm to the touch. My mother went stiff as a board; she stared at his hand, but it didn't budge. She then stared so vehemently that his hand removed itself and returned to the other in the gap between his knees. She breathed again and so did I.

So, he said to me, what's going on?

She's impossible, my mother said, pulling at a rough edge of her nail.

He spoke to me in Afrikaans, tender words spoken in a way almost maternal. Wat makeer? What's the matter? Again, at this intimacy, which excluded her, my mother stiffened, turning her lips into a pale pink ribbon.

Look, Dan said, addressing my mother directly, she doesn't want to go to England. She's scared she won't fit in, she's a bush girl; she's one of us now. It's too late to try and turn her into an Englisher. He leaned towards my mother and she pulled back. Look now, he said again, she's right there in the middle of her studies, so why can't she stay on, with Angela, and finish her matric also? It's only a couple more years.

It's out of the question.

She can come here for the holidays; it's no trouble to us. We'd love to have her.

I knew my mother was getting angry, but he didn't seem to click to that as he kept on putting forward his reasons, trying to get round her by being lighthearted. All the while she became more tense and anxious, until, abruptly, she stood up. No, she said, she's coming with us. Her passage is booked. It's too late now. Gerald wouldn't hear of it. Hearing her say that, the finality of it: the passage booked, his not hearing of it, I knew it was over. There was no point in trying to enlist my mother's help. Poor thing, she was as helpless as I was. I'd already tried speaking to my father, when I first heard that we were going. At the time, when I made what I thought were some rather good suggestions about what I might do after I'd matriculated from St Mary's – like being a journalist, or going to university – he'd scoffed, looked at me and said, you'll never amount to anything, wherever you are. So there it was. I could have bolted, as once I would have – and certainly the hot little room, with my mother standing in anger, and Dan, lounging, was enough to make me want to, and so it was only later that I actually realized that I'd done something different. I hadn't clattered out of there like a crazy person, trampling everything in my path. I'd sat them out, and in the end it was they who left, and I could feel a little in charge of myself for once.

When they'd gone, I turned my face to the wall, and, scratching with my nail on its roughness, I decided to put walls all around me, high, unassailable walls. I'd make a fortress so that no one could get me, and that way I'd be able to go on. I wanted to go to the store to see Rena, to sit beside her and hold the wool, letting it run through my fingers as she knitted. I wanted it to be the way it used to be. Even the thought of it filled me with tears. But I was on my own now. I stayed away because I loved her and she loved me back. I couldn't risk love any more.

Later, around noon, when I went out beyond the barns and past the kraal, I sat at the dam, throwing stones out across the brown water, and it seemed to me that everything was holding still, and because nothing moved and nothing changed, it was eternal. I loved it so much that I thought I'd die if I lost it. And then it came to me that I'd always loved it this way because I'd had nothing else to love. The cooing doves fell asleep in the trees, the sun pounded down on the water, a hawk swooped up into an eddy of air and hovered there, not stirring. The world was even, balanced. Oxen moved like archaic beasts and the little boys trailed after the goats, leading them out to the grasses. I sat there all day, not moving, just staring out across the water, watching and waiting.

I stayed there until the moon was high; half of the moon was missing that night and the sky was wide and silent as the reaches of pale dead grass. Softly a few sounds stirred between the trees, and dark shadows appeared in the blue half-light. The eyes of wild animals made stars between the grasses; a bat swooped; a hyena gave its mournful cry. There was a smell in the wind, indescribable – achingly familiar – home, home.

In England would I ever see stars with all that smog and fog? And, anyway, there were no stars on earth as beautiful as the stars that looked down on Africa. How could I live without seeing the long golden spires of moonlight turn liquid and pour down on the fields at night? How could I breathe if this air was taken from me? I seemed to see the English sky, as I'd seen it in pictures and paintings: the endless grey of it, the buildings shoved together; the cramped gardens overlooking railway tracks, washing on lines drying in the smoke. And because it was such a little place, with so many people jammed into it, the sky could only be a distant patch between rooftops, with air that was lifeless and flat. I'd lived all my life where the air was buoyant and spicy, in a place picked clean as a carcass. What would I do in a world of identical houses, made up of small rooms, lace-curtained windows and locked doors?

My mother had told me things about England. She began to do it more. She started clearing out her cupboards and putting clothes in piles around the room. No one will polish your shoes for you there, she said, holding up a striped dress for a moment before hurling it into the corner. Oh no, and you won't be having nice clean clothes every day. And don't imagine I will wash and iron them for you. You'll have to wash up and tidy up after yourself, and of course we'll have to find a boarding school that will take you. When she was less scared, she'd be bossy and brisk; other times she'd sound brave and hopeful. Well, you know, dear, it will be a relief to go out in the countryside and see grass that is actually green, and I'm sure I can find help, of some kind, and a nice house – though the houses will feel small, I'm sure, and the windows and doors won't be like these – because of the cold, you know, but there will be nice fires, of course. But oh, I wonder who will bring in the coal, and who'll clean the grate? She'd become agitated and anxious and I'd have to step in and make up a whole lot of rubbish to get that awful look off her face.

She'd started off grandly enough. Your father is being transferred to the Commonwealth Relations Office in Whitehall, she announced. And with these words, her snootiness, somewhat in hiding while she was uncertain about the future, came back in full force. She smartened up her accent and sounded more la-di-da. Peering intently at the mirror, and dabbing lemon juice on the stray freckle, she'd say, do you think it's true, you know, what the natives say about Pond's Vanishing Cream? What's that? I'd ask, running a finger over the mahogany surface of her dressing table, writing in the fine dust of her face powder as if it were sand. Oh, you know, that it gets rid of blackness. That's why they use it, of course; they think it makes their skin whiter. I'd say that it was worth a try, but I assured her that really I couldn't see a single freckle on her face, and anyway I thought freckles were nice because I had some.

Oh no, she said, freckles are vulgar, definitely. Now, pass me that cream, dear, and let's see if it works.

She'd begin wondering what kind of clothes she'd need, how much entertaining there'd be, and whether they'd keep in touch with people they'd known in the B.P. But soon the worry and uncertainty of it all made her fretful. How much would help cost? How would she manage to do everything – to clean a house, cook, wash and iron. How was that even done? She'd been brought up in India; she knew nothing about that kind of thing. You know, dear, I wasn't brought up to do those kinds of things, or to work. I wasn't even taught how to look nice, I had to teach myself that. As she kept telling me what to expect in England, she frightened us both, but she couldn't stop. People who have gone back say what an unfriendly place it is, she'd say nervously. You can live in a street for years and nobody will speak to you. You can die in your bed and not be found for days. People who'd left for good said they always missed the good old B.P. – no servants, no parties, no fun – and drink and cigarettes a terrible price – how did anyone manage at all? She would pace up and down, almost wringing her hands, and in the end all I could do was to make her some tea and suggest that perhaps she should have a little lie-down to make herself feel better.

She made it clear to me that my time at home was almost up. Oh, you won't live with us for long, she said, sipping her tea. You'll go and live by yourself, probably in London. I don't think we'd be able to afford a house in London ourselves, but you could get a room, or a bed-sitter, or something. You'll have to get a job. Girls need to have something they can fall back on – typing or nursing, something like that – in case things go wrong, so they're not stranded if their husband dies, or runs off. Don't expect us to look after you once your schooling is over.

So I knew how my future would be: I'd live in a bed-sitting-room with peeling wallpaper and exhausted, dirty furniture and feed shillings into the meter to keep the gas fire going, or to heat my soup. I'd work in a dingy office as a secretary and have someone boss me around all day, and have me go out and get him a sandwich for his lunch, as if I were a servant. Out of the window would be the grey sky and the smog, and the people would walk around in heavy coats and would barely smile because it was so cold. My mother had made it plain, and for a few minutes I believed her. I thought that's how it would be. But something else was stirred into the misery, just a couple of words that made me feel differently: Fight back. I hung on to them for dear life.

That last night on the le Cordeur farm, I knew that I wouldn't come back; I looked at it as if I was trying to burn it into memory, seal it in time. But it wouldn't keep still for me. The farm, and the very land that it stood on, was sway-ing and moving in time. I couldn't hold it back. It would go its own way without me. Standing on the steps leading up to the L-shaped house, I seemed to see it as it would be in the years after we'd all gone. The rooms would be empty and sand would drift in and form little piles in the corners. The windows would crack and the walls would cave in. Screen doors would creak in the wind, the way they had at Bunny Swart's house that day, and wild birds would roost in the rafters below the corrugated roof where once rain had thundered down, sounding like a drunk dancing on the rooftop. The lovely mansions of our brief occupation would crumble and fall, becoming shelter for wild creatures and homeless refugees. In the hospitals, nurses would still walk around in the dark blue uniforms and snow-white caps of the Empire; children would walk to school in white shirts and pinafores like the ones we'd once worn, but we wouldn't be there to see them. And, looking behind them, they'd have no memory of who we were, or why we came, or left, or even why we loved them the way we did.

Seventeen

ANGELA WAS ALLOWED TO STAY ON AT ST MARY'S TO FINISH her matric, but my mother, my father, Susan and I took the train to Cape Town. We'd lived at the Cape before, for those six-month stretches, but this time when I saw the sea, rippled and lovely, fathomless and deep, it meant nothing to me. When I stared at the horizon, it was as if I was trying to see over it to the little island in the fog that was our destination. A deep coldness settled on my heart and even the rippling heat couldn't warm me as I stood on the quay, looking up at the white bulk of the boat that would soon carry us away. This time, the ship that was to take us to England wasn't a floating palace with a royal house for its name. It bore no scarlet and black funnel, nor did it have the lovely lines of the Union-Castle boats, those lilac-blue planes that would dip and rise in the heavy swell of the Cape rollers. We were sailing on MV *Jagersfontein*, of the Holland-Afrika line, a serviceable black and white ship with straight sides.

As we were walking up the gangplank, with streamers blowing in the wind and a band playing 'Auld Lang Syne', I suddenly panicked and grabbed my mother's arm. We've left Angela behind, I howled. She should've come with us, the way we came out to Africa together. I was desperate, pulling at her. How could I be going on without her, when usually she'd gone on ahead, to make the way easier for me? I wanted to run back down the gangplank and get her. My mother shook me off. Oh, don't be so silly, she said, just get up there and stop making a fuss. You're holding everyone up. Oh, for heaven's sake, what is there to be crying about at a time like this? Pull yourself together and hurry up about it. What is the matter with you? Don't you know that we're going Home?

So I went on without Angela. I stood on the deck, leaning over the railing, as the boat pulled slowly out of Table Bay, escorted by the desolate clangour of the bells on the buoys. We seemed to pass under the mountains, and as we left port we seemed to sink deeper into the sea. Gulls followed in our wake. Streamers came flying out over the water, and we caught them if we could, but soon they'd snapped or fallen on to the water. The people down below us on the quayside kept waving goodbye, becoming smaller as we moved slowly out of the bay and headed for open water. The streamers floated for a moment on the sea and then drowned. The foghorns were bagpipes at the edge of a grave.

As the ship sailed away, and the bay widened into the Southern Ocean, Table Mountain loomed, flat and flinty as the colours of the bush, becoming darker with distance. I looked behind me at the mountain ranges, and at the bay that was growing smaller as we kept on going. Soon, the African seabirds following in the foam and the spray returned to their perches on the rocks. Their cries grew muffled and then all natural sound ceased. Our engines roared, and the tugboat that had escorted us out turned back; the pilot gave a wave and returned to the shore. Slowly, the waves flattened out and the white hull ploughed steadily on, dividing the waves, leaving a churning maelstrom in its wake. Now we were alone and unescorted. We were heading back to the equator and then north. I stood looking over the rail, and for a moment I weakened, and turned once more my head. It was still there, in all its majesty, the blue bulk of the peninsula with its sheltering mountains, with its southeasters blowing, taking us away, taking us away.

That night, my mother was dancing in a black dress with white specks all over a wide skirt, her tiny waist sleek as a wasp's. As she swirled, she left the crackle and hiss of taffeta in her wake, and the heady scent of Chanel No. 5. But though she was dancing with my father, she appeared, as she always did, to be dancing alone. My father didn't notice and, though he was still the one not drinking, he was on good form, certain this time of his place, heading for Whitehall and the corridors of power. I can see him on the boat. He'd recovered himself a little, this posting had restored him, but he'd done it by relinquishing, as entirely as he could, what he really was: by now, he was an Irishman quite stripped of any of that unfortunate native Irishness so unappealing to the English. He'd been moulded by the rigours of the colonies, and he'd learned his place by his dependency on the benevolence of his superiors at the Colonial Office. He'd become an Englishman, adopting or aping their attitudes, so much so that you could say that England had neutered him. So he stood there, making small talk with the other men, talking of his plans, watching the band play on, anticipating that soon he'd be reaping his reward: perhaps a knighthood, but surely an Order of the British Empire, that at least. Had you told him then that he'd never see Africa again, as he'd never seen India again, he'd have said bloody rubbish. And if you'd suggested that in a couple of years he'd be out of the service altogether, jobless and futureless, he wouldn't have believed it for a minute.

The passengers were knocking it back like there was no tomorrow – an endless supply of gin and whisky, with stewards always on hand to keep the glasses brimming. They were riding the crest of a wave, many of them leaving Africa for good, heading for distant places: Australia or America, countries where the good life was still possible. Their voices were loud and enthusiastic. They'd got out before the stampede and were sailing towards safety and a new future. Africa was altogether too risky now. The political atmosphere was electric – revolutionaries demanding change and an iron-fisted government and police state suppressing all protest in the south. It wasn't too long before Sharpeville, when the South African Police mowed down sixty-nine blacks during a peaceful demonstration. It was the beginning of house arrests, treason trials and life imprisonments. It was the time of fighting back. Our fellow passengers were fleeing the country early, getting out before the last piece of Africa blew.

We sailed away from all of it and retreated into the sealed world of the ship. I could see how immediately we began to recreate the spirit of the bush on the ship. Everyone was on borrowed time, out for a spell, on a tour of duty, or between things, so the same things happened. Men and women, isolated from past and present, hurled themselves into each other's arms with wild abandon. Passionate shipboard romances sprang up overnight, lush and febrile in the sun-drenched air. Lovers walked arm in arm on deserted moon-washed decks, and kissed long and hard while the bright stars rushed across the sky. You could catch them at it – a man last seen dancing with his wife on the polished parquet floor lay sprawled over the mute body of a woman last seen in second class. A young Englishman going home to marry his childhood sweetheart lay tangled in the nets on the crew-only deck with a steward out on his maiden voyage. There was a suicide too: a coffin folded up in the Union Jack was lowered slowly into the ocean as we recited the Twenty-third Psalm.

We sailed on northward, and passed the equator, but there was no ceremony this time: we just crossed the line and kept going. But, although no ceremony took place, there was an echo of the old voyages. One day, as we approached the equator, the crew – once natty in their sharp whites with gold braid – came down dressed in black from top to toe. It seemed that the lower the sun dipped in the sky, the more we drifted into shadow and gloom. The sea was no longer aqua, and the waves were heavy and deep. When the sun came out, the shadow of the ship fell upon the waters, and it followed us like an albatross, leading us closer and closer to Home. The days dropped off, one by one, as on we sailed, and as the days passed, the climate and the light shifted dramatically. The air became flat and cold, the light thickened. Woollies came out from the hold, and people could be seen walking the decks in overcoats and hats. As we turned our faces towards England, we knew we were leaving the new world behind and crossing back into the old, and we became sombre and quiet, leaning over the rails, staring out to sea. The water was green and glassy, but it was so still that it seemed barely to move, and the ship itself seemed motionless on the sea.

As we came closer to England, I saw that it was flat, the way it looked on the atlas. It didn't have the lovely, rounded pear-shape of Africa, with its southern peninsula jutting into the sea: the fairest Cape, the Cape of Storms, the Cape of Good Hope. England lay quietly in the water, a painted island on a painted ocean, and seeing it that way, the white cliffs low and crooked, it seemed such a little place, and so grey and dismal. When we pulled into the docks at Southampton, I saw a huge signboard, showing a glass of beer, and across it was written: TAKE COURAGE.

Epilogue

TEN YEARS AGO, WHEN AFRICA AND MY LIFE THERE WAS NO more than a dream, a day came when a storm broke in my head. I woke with a headache that wouldn't let up and I was aware of acute anxiety running up and down my body like a current. I was shaky, subject to sudden alarms, unable to concentrate or think straight. This had been going on for some time, probably starting soon after my father's death some years before, but in the previous six months it had been getting worse. My old nightmares had come back, and odd, quick images like hallucinations: a bowl filling with blood, a child's voice crying when no child was there, and then one day I looked down at my feet and saw little black Mary Janes in place of my high-heeled shoes. Just for a split second. The image was there, and then it was gone, just like the other images. I was terrified. It was the madness come back to me, I was certain of it, and

244

I didn't know where it was leading. I wanted to try to sleep the headache off, but I also had a strong premonition that I might start screaming and not be able to stop. A scream was lodged in my throat; it had been there all my life, but now it seemed to be trying to get out.

I went up to the third floor of my house and climbed into an old brass bed. It lives in the spare bedroom – a large, airy room with pale walls and wide, golden floorboards. Tall trees outside the windows keep the room shaded and quiet, and it feels a little like our old tree house in Maun because it's so high up, nestled in among heavy branches and cooled by the winds. I think of it as my summer bedroom and I often migrate there when the weather's hot; the morning doves come close to the windows at dawn and you hear their calls before they retire for the night.

I was in that strange place just before sleep and oblivion, when the mind begins to hover over images in a way that lacks sequence or sense. I was under the covers – it was cold, or I was cold – I don't know which, but it was at this point that I began to suffocate, for no reason at all. I started thrashing about in the bed, gasping for air, and then I sat bolt upright and I had the strongest feeling that I'd thrown something off my face. The sense of suffocation was still there and my heart was thumping so hard that it was causing me pain. I was hyperventilating by now. I knew that I was having a panic attack. I tried to take control of myself. I ordered myself to breathe. I talked myself down, and the minute I closed my eyes, I fell asleep.

When I woke, after about twenty minutes, there was an image stuck in my head. It came from a dream I kept having of a man without a face. I could see the man's body, but in the dream he didn't have a face. It was a bit like film footage when they blur out the identity of the person being interviewed. The image reminded me of the nightmares of my childhood when I seemed to see a face without features, sometimes standing in the shadows at the end of my bed, sometimes staring at me out of the darkness of a dream. The thought of a man without a face wouldn't get out of my mind, however calmly or rationally I thought about it, but pretty soon I couldn't think at all. I was adrift in the pale room with the afternoon light filtering through the windows. I felt removed, very far away, very small and depersonalized and in a state of suspension: no feeling was coming through. Then the suffocation came back and now it felt very bad, as if I was dying for lack of air.

And then, quite simply, I wasn't there at all. I was very small, six years old, and I was lying in my bed in Swaziland, listening to the hum of the electricity generator, waiting for it to stutter out and for my night-light to vanish into the darkness with everything else: the end of my bed, the shape of the window, the cupboard with toys on top of it. The door opened a crack and there was light beneath it, which must have come from the moonlight – a thin, golden line, which, for a second, my eye caught and held. Then I was suffocating again. I could smell the Sunlight Soap that was used to wash our clothes in the tub; it was coming from the pillow over my face and I could smell the feathers. I could feel the spokes of the feathers sticking into my mouth and face. I started to thrash about, trying to find a small channel of air so that I wouldn't be smothered, jerking my head around and kicking with my legs. There was a shaft of excruciating pain that shot right up the centre of my body. I split. And then it was as if I could see myself, as if from far away. I had no head because the pillow was over it. I could see the top of my body wearing pale yellow pyjamas with ducks on and white piping around the cuffs and collar. I couldn't see the rest of my body, but I could feel it. And then I couldn't feel it at all.

When I came to, my teeth were chattering, but they didn't feel like my teeth at all. They felt like my milk teeth used to feel, light porcelain with little ridges, and I thought that if I couldn't stop them from chattering against one another like that they might fall out of my head. Everything inside my body felt loose as if an explosion had gone off inside it, knocking my organs and bones around. I was shaking and then I realized that I was bleeding, and when I felt between my legs my fingers were covered with blood. I began sobbing and I couldn't stop. I was shaking and I couldn't stop. I screamed once and then went silent and I lay there like the dead thing that I was.

The rest came back to me, clear and simple, just as it had happened, just as it had been there all the time – forgotten but not forgotten, known but not known – just waiting to come back all those years. It was dawn and I was lying in my bed in Swaziland. Angela was walking across to my bed from the door and she brought me a small glass of milk. I took a sip, and the sweet lactic taste of it filled me with horror. I couldn't drink it. I haven't had a glass of milk since: can't stand the taste, won't touch it, neat, in a glass like that. No idea why I felt that way. Just hated milk. I got out of bed when I could hear the servants moving around in the kitchen, and I knew that he'd gone to work. I went to the bathroom and it was like peeing through broken glass. I looked in the bowl and it was full of blood; it seemed to be rising slowly up the sides. My pyjamas were covered with blood, and so was I. I went to my mother because I didn't know what else to do. She took one look at me, and her face contorted. What have you done to yourself? I was confused by the question. I said, Dad did it.

She moved into a breathless hysteria; she was swept up into it until she was angrier than I'd ever seen her, or would see her again. Don't you EVER tell a lie like that again, she screamed, grabbing my shoulders and shaking me. Do you hear me? Never, ever say that again.

She hauled me off to the bath, dragging me by one arm, then ran the water hard and told me to wash myself. She pulled the sheets off the bed and got me out of the bath so that she could put them in. She filled the tub with cold water till it was close to overflowing. The water was pink. I watched it. I watched her. She wasn't talking now. Angela wasn't there. I couldn't see her anywhere. Later, my mother took me to the doctor. I don't know what she told him. He lived down the road from us, and normally he was quite friendly. On this day though he didn't speak to me, and when he did speak, it was to my mother. Children, he said, stitching me up without any anaesthesia, don't have any feelings down there. We went home, my mother and I, and we never spoke about it again.

When I came down from the third floor, I was no longer myself. It was as if I'd been sent off to Goedgegun. It was all over and nothing would be the same again. I was a ghost for the rest of that Saturday, a speechless, wandering presence, barely able to communicate what had happened and too afraid to try, because if I did I'd be breaking my mother's prohibition. I was spooked all the time – jumpy – the way I am right this minute, writing this, only a whole lot worse. I was terrified of the dark all over again. I was marooned in the past, and I was way out of my body, adrift in a trance world where I could operate in my daily life, barely, while not being there at all. Just as it was when I was little, as it had always been.

For a while I believed that it had just happened once. I needed to believe that. But as more pieces fell into place, as memory fragments came together and the half-known became known, it was more than the mind could bear. It took me months to get over the aftershocks, and images kept floating up out of nowhere, shattering the composure of my life. For a year I was completely out of my mind, out of time – gone. I found myself being self-destructive again, as I'd been in Africa, and later in England during all those years of homesickness and misery after I'd left Africa. I was living my life like a somnambulist and I couldn't get out of the way of danger when I needed to. I could get into trouble just crossing a road. I began walking into cars the way I'd done in Mafeking, and once I stood at the open window on the top floor, as I'd done at St Mary's, and thought, shall I go? And, if I hadn't been married to someone who could both witness and endure this time, I mightn't be here at all. And then, slowly, slowly, for all of the horror and suffering, something else emerged from the hidden story: a diamond had been forming in the darkness, and when it came to light, my whole life made sense to me. For the first time, I'd got the whole picture.

I went to England to speak to Angela.

She'd been living there since she'd left St Mary's after completing her matric. She'd trained and taken up a nursing career at the Charing Cross Hospital in London, and by the time I went to see her she'd been at the hospital for almost twenty years, devoting herself to patients suffering from breathlessness and respiratory disease. She'd taken on the nursing cause itself: pitching her strong will against tyranny, and fighting hierarchy with a fury that could send people reeling. She was still working there when I went to see her. I stayed in her house in Ealing, and for days I tried to bring up the subject of the past, of our childhood, of all that had come back to me. But I couldn't. Every time I tried, it was as if a hand whammed across my mouth and shut me up. I couldn't say a word.

One evening Ange and I were in the kitchen, and I was looking out of the window at the garden wall and the tangled vines of moonflowers that had bloomed in the summer. The table was set and we were about to have dinner. Her husband and daughter were in the dining-room waiting for us. Ange tipped the rice into a bowl, and with her other hand she passed me a bunch of parsley. I looked at it and I thought my heart would break as I remembered how the parsley grew under the tap in the garden in Gabs, and how it was always green because the tap dripped, and if not for that, it wouldn't have survived at all.

I looked at her and tried again to tell her, and I couldn't. My jaw locked. I kept trying and I kept failing. Finally I burst out and said, There's something I came here to tell you, but now I'm here I can't seem to tell you. I keep trying to say it, but I can't. She took one look at me and said, It's incest, isn't it?

We went right in to dinner and we both managed to eat it. The four of us had a perfectly normal meal, as if nothing had happened at all. That's how it was, how it had always been. We knew the ropes. One morning, years and years before, I'd sat at another table, while my father was eating his breakfast and drinking his tea, just like a normal person, and I, just like a normal child, was sitting in front of my unbroken boiled egg. I was in a trance, barely there at all, and my mother was getting impatient. She reached across and swatted the top off my egg, and said, Get on with it, hurry up. I picked up my spoon and stuck it into the soft-boiled egg and looked inside at the milky, slimy, moving white of the barely cooked egg. I lifted a spoonful and the slime slid off the spoon and into my mouth. I couldn't breathe. I couldn't swallow. I'd rather have died than swallow. I vomited all over myself and the egg and spoon, and the vomit landed in my lap, all over my pleated green gymslip.

We got back to the subject, Ange and I. We might have left it at that spare exchange in her kitchen, but she took me back to it, she found a time when we could be alone, and she asked me to tell her what happened. I didn't tell her much, because I could tell that she didn't want to know much. I told her just about the first time, in Swaziland when I was six and she was eight. No details. Nothing for the mind to get hooked and snared on. But when I told her about being taken to the doctor, she looked at me with a startled flash of memory, and being a nurse, always having been a nurse, she said, I remember that bleed.

And that was the end of it. We put it away and we haven't said much about it since, nothing more about what actually happened, nothing about the consequences, or about how much it has affected her. She made it clear to me that she didn't want to excavate further, and certainly not on her own behalf. She said to me, wearily, you were always willing to go down into the dark without a candle, but I'm not. So we took up our lives and we went on, trying to make a new surface over the old rutted road, trying to hold together by remembering the beauty. She and I are the last two left of our original family of five: our mother died first, then our father, and then, two years ago, our youngest sister, Susan, died too. We're the last witnesses, Angela and I, of a childhood that, after all this time, seems to be part of a landscape that has gone – as inevitable and sad as that. Each one of us – my mother, my father, my sisters and I – survived as best we could, in the place that we happened to have found ourselves in, which was beautiful beyond words.

The life we had is gone now and the places of our childhood no longer exist – Bechuanaland, Rhodesia, the Belgian Congo – they've all gone, along with white supremacy and the cool glamour of colonial certainty. That life vanished into time as quickly as those names were tossed off the map – so quickly that there's barely a record of all that happened there, and all that it meant. I used to suffer at the idea of being among people who wouldn't know where I'd come from and what I'd seen. How could I tell them of the beauty of Africa? How could I show them the magic of the river in Maun and the African women walking down to the fields with their babies strapped to their backs? How could I tell them of egrets sailing the sky above the lily-laden waters of the Thamalakane River? What could they know of the silence of the bush when the ghost of the Bushman came loping by? Or how the moonlight caught on the long spears of the acacia trees and flooded the desert with silver? How could I tell them any of it?

Now I see that no one place is more beautiful than another, and beauty belongs to anyone who loves it. The polished light of America has come from Africa and will make its way to Havana and Helsinki before landing back in God's lap. The cool wind blowing in from the Caribbean is shot with spice, and the summer storm hurls down rain pretty much the same way in Honolulu and Tibet as it does in Gaberones. The sunlight in Guatemala is as tender as it is in Sussex, and mountains have surfaced from the collisions of continents in India just as they have in the Karoo. A flower born for a day is as much part of the loveliness of the earth in Siberia as it is in the Kalahari. These days, substitutes will do.